Hope for Today

365 Devotions for Depression & Anxiety

BroadStreet
PUBLISHING

BroadStreet Publishing Group, LLC.
Savage, Minnesota, USA
Broadstreetpublishing.com

Hope for Today

© 2020 by BroadStreet Publishing®

978-1-4245-6101-8 (faux leather)
978-1-4245-6102-5 (eBook)

Devotional entries composed by Sara Perry.

Design by Chris Garborg | garborgdesign.com
Editorial services by Michelle Winger | literallyprecise.com

Printed in China.

20 21 22 23 24 25 26 7 6 5 4 3 2 1

The LORD your God is living among you.

He is a mighty savior.

He will take delight in you with gladness.

With his love, he will calm all your fears.

He will rejoice over you with joyful songs.

ZEPHANIAH 3:17 NLT

Introduction

The circumstances of life may have you feeling anxious, overwhelmed, discouraged, or even depressed. Isn't it encouraging to know that God's love is not dependent on your situation? Because his love for you is unchanging and his promises are true, you can choose to believe that today will be a good day.

Find the hope, joy, and strength that is abundant in God as you reflect on these devotional entries, Scriptures, and prayers. No matter what comes your way, you can get through it with God at your side. He will never leave you. His unending mercy and grace are always waiting for you.

Rest in the compassion of your good Father. He listens to every word you utter, and he fully understands your heart.

January

The LORD hears his people
when they call to him for help.
He rescues them from all their troubles.

PSALM 34:17 NLT

Never Alone

The Lord himself will go before you.
He will be with you;
he will not leave you or forget you.
Don't be afraid and don't worry.

DEUTERONOMY 31:8 NCV

Nowhere in the Bible does it say that we are to strive to do things on our own. In fact, the Word repeatedly reminds us that God partners with the weak and willing and gives them strength. God often meets us where we feel the most vulnerable.

What areas of weakness are you facing right now? Where does fear threaten to keep you immobile? He is with you in the midst of your greatest triumph and your greatest struggle. He has not forgotten about you. He has made a way for you where you have felt confusion and angst. Let go of the worry today and trust that he is at work in the details of your life—every single one of them!

Holy Spirit, I invite you into my weakness today. Give me eyes to see what you are doing as I cling to you. Thank you that I am not alone in any situation. Help me to remember today, above all else, that you are with me.

Unchanging One

Why are you in despair, O my soul?
And why have you become disturbed within me?
Hope in God, for I shall yet praise Him,
the help of my countenance and my God.

PSALM 42:11 NASB

We are not immune to feeling discouragement and despair. God, the lifter of our heads, is the source of all the help we need in every season of the soul. When anxiety fills our bodies and worries overshadow the goodness in our lives, we can turn to our good Father who never changes.

When we feel overwhelmed by the worries of this life, let's take a moment to breathe and direct our soul's gaze to the one who sees all and is over all. Though we cannot control what will happen in this world, we can focus our hearts on who God is, always has been, and will continue to be.

God, my help, fill me today with your Spirit. Breathe new life into my weary soul, causing hope to rise once again. I fix the eyes of my heart on your goodness and faithfulness for you never fail!

Delivered

*Every time they cried out to you in their despair,
you were faithful to deliver them;
you didn't disappoint them.*

PSALM 22:5 TPT

We are not promised a pain-free life. No such thing exists! When we face trials and circumstances that oppose our hopes and expectations, what do we do with the desperation we feel? We can come to God with everything, including our fears, anxieties, and doubts.

There is no human experience that is outside of Jesus' understanding and no situation that is out of God's reach. When was the last time you cried out to God from a desperate place? Have you been honest with God and yourself? Don't hold back; you may just find that, in his faithfulness, he will not disappoint you.

Faithful One, I come to you with an open heart today. Let your light shine on the places I have kept hidden from you; I cry out from the depths of my soul for you to rescue me. Meet me in the middle of my mess, bringing order to the chaos. I trust you.

Steady

He lifted me out of the pit of despair,
out of the mud and the mire.
He set my feet on solid ground
and steadied me as I walked along.

PSALM 40:2 NLT

Do you feel like you're drowning under the weight of your circumstances? When darkness makes it hard to see where you're going, what keeps you from sinking into desperation? You were never meant to rely on your own limited resources to get out of tough situations.

Where you have felt stuck, cry out to God for help. Invite him into the specific places that overwhelm you and watch how he lifts you out of the muck and sets your feet on solid ground. He can do it, and he is faithful to meet you no matter what kind of mess you find yourself in. He rescues his beloved children over and over again.

Father God, I need your help. Show up in my life with your resurrection power, bringing life out of what has felt like death. Fill my heart with hope as I watch your faithfulness unfold before my very eyes.

Hopeful Heart

Anxiety weighs down the heart,
but a kind word cheers it up.
PROVERBS 12:25 NIV

When the worries of life weigh down your soul, what do you do? Do you try to soldier on and just get through the day? It is exhausting to try to keep it together when anxiety is coursing through your body.

God is full of kindness and so much gentler than we expect. If we come to him with our burdens, he is faithful to take the weight of them and help us. He never turns away; he does not need to take time to consider whether it's worth it, for his love knows no limits. We can never reach the end of his incredible kindness. Have you known God in this way? If it feels too good to be true, you've stumbled into the goodness of God. He is always better than you expect.

Kind Father, I so easily forget the nature of your goodness especially toward me. Lift the weight of my anxious thoughts and bring peace and clarity to my mind. Fill my body with your love that casts out every fear. May my heart once again know the joy of loving you.

Unbothered

*They do not worry about how short life is,
because God keeps them busy with what they love to do.*
ECCLESIASTES 5:20 NCV

How have you been using your time? In this day and age, it's so easy to get swept up in the digital world and to pass time without considering what we are filling it with. If you were intentional about doing things you love, what would that look like?

We have one short life on this earth. How we spend our time reflects how we live. Whether intentionally or not, the time passes. Will we live our lives with resolution, our eyes fixed on a goal, or will we just let it pass without engaging in our purpose? God is masterful in his plans. If we yield our lives to him, he is faithful to direct us.

Lord, you hold all my days. You see the end from the beginning and every space in between. I offer you my life again. Restore meaning where I have felt aimless. Ease the worries of my mind with your boundless grace. Your ways are so much better than my own, and you know me better than I know myself. Lead me, Lord.

Shielded

You, O LORD, are a shield about me,
my glory, and the lifter of my head.

PSALM 3:3 ESV

When storms of life rage, where can we find shelter? God's Word says that he is our help in times of trouble. We can rely on him to guard us and keep us secure. He shields us from the fiery darts of the enemy—the lies that distort our true identity as sons and daughters of the Most High.

When the chaos of life makes it hard to see up from down, God is a steady rock to stand on. His Word is unfailing, and all his promises come to pass. Have you been keeping your head down just trying to survive? God, the lifter of your head, is your strong help. He holds onto you when you don't have the strength to reach out to him. Lift your eyes to his gaze today, and you will see a loving Father who will never let you go.

God my strength, when I am worn down from the hits that life gives, I need you to hold me up. Be my defender; I can't fight these battles on my own. I don't even want to. You, Lord, are faithful and I trust you. Cover me with your love as I lean into your arms today.

Resilient

We are hard pressed on every side, but not crushed;
perplexed, but not in despair.

2 CORINTHIANS 4:8 NIV

When the storms of life are harsh and seem unending, we have an opportunity to make a choice. We can either give into despair or hold onto hope, which will cause us to persevere. We don't do this on our own; rather, we rely on the Holy Spirit who continually fills us with the love of God. It is this unrelenting love that has the strength to overpower every fear.

What is overwhelming in your life right now? Have your thoughts been overcome with worry? Fix your eyes on Jesus Christ and remember his life of love that overcame death and destruction. Your inheritance is life!

Jesus, when I look at your life, I see the evidence of love beyond my greatest imaginings. I set my gaze on you today, remembering that you have overcome the world. With your life in mine, I can overcome too.

Kingdom Bearer

*He has delivered us from the power of darkness
and conveyed us into the kingdom of the Son of His love.*
COLOSSIANS 1:13 NKJV

God is deliverer and protector. In him, we find that we are both kept secure and freed to move in liberty. We have been brought from darkness into light, where everything is made clear. Where there seemed to be no way, God made a way for us to be restored in full connection with him through Jesus.

His love never fails. It is the driving force of all creation and what fuels the restoration work he is constantly doing. We belong to a kingdom of love, full of compassion and mercy. There is plenty of room for the weak and the humble; those who struggle always have access to the strength of God through his grace. There is never a circumstance too difficult or a problem too great that God does not already have a solution. As we look to him, we will find that we bear his signature. We have been marked by love.

God over all, you are my deliverer. When I don't know where to turn and confusion threatens to immobilize me, you step in with your peace and your steady hand guides me. You are full of compassion at every point. Thank you for your deliverance. I depend on you still!

Sweet Words

Kind words are like honey—
sweet to the soul
and healthy for the body.
PROVERBS 16:24 NLT

It is amazing how a kind word can crack the hard layer of a heart that is prone to protect itself. When sweet, genuine words are spoken, they build up our souls and encourage our hearts. Proverbs says that they even bring health to our bodies!

When you consider your thought life and the words you speak over yourself, do they reflect the kindness with which your heavenly Father speaks over you? Sometimes it is easier to be kinder to others, but grace given must also be grace received. Do you treat yourself with the same kindness you would treat your loved ones? If not, today is a good day to reconsider your worth.

Holy Spirit, I ask for your awareness today to know what it is that God thinks of me. In light of his great love, give me the grace to be kind to myself, as intentionally loving and patient as I would be with a child. I want to see myself through eyes of love the way you do.

Confidence

*Faith is confidence in what we hope for
and assurance about what we do not see.*
HEBREWS 11:1 NIV

There is so much change in our lives on a regular basis. It is difficult to know what we can cling to in a world that is always shifting. When it comes down to it, what are the unshakeable tenets of our faith? God, in his love, makes it clear that he is unchanging. Our understanding of his goodness may fluctuate, sometimes multiple times a day, but his character remains constant.

Where does your confidence lie? Are you relying on your own intelligence, strength, and determination to succeed in life? When all else fails, what is left for you to hold onto? If you don't have an answer for that, let your heart open to the Spirit of wisdom who conveys the mysteries of God to those who ask.

Unchanging One, you are the only constant in a continuously changing world. I ask for your perspective on my life today; I want to see things from your point of view. Let my confidence be in you, not found in something that will inevitably shift. All my hope is in you.

Freedom

We have freedom now,
because Christ made us free.
So stand strong.
Do not change
and go back into the slavery of the law.

GALATIANS 5:1 NCV

The beautiful reality of the Gospel is that Jesus sacrificed his life so we would be free from the chains of sin and death. He paved a way to the Father so nothing would keep us from him again. Nothing. No hardship, no struggle, no addiction, no wrongs done to us. Nothing can keep us from his great love.

Are you living in the reality of this great freedom? You have the choice to live unbound with nothing holding you back from God's persistent grace. You have been welcomed into God's family as a dearly loved child. You are not a weird, estranged cousin in the family of God; you are his. You belong to him. No wall, no chains, no fear, and no doubt can keep you from him. He has set you free. So, be free.

God, your relentless grace has covered my life and set me free to choose my way. My past does not dictate my future, nor do my struggles get to direct my life. I align myself with you and your kingdom today. May your freedom reign in my life, opening up what was once restricted.

Filled

From his fullness
we have all received, grace upon grace.
JOHN 1:16 NRSV

In the whirlwind of life, it is so easy to feel depleted. There is always more to do, further needs to be met, and seemingly endless demands on our attention and time. We were never intended to live in a constant state of lack. Our God is full of abundance with everything we could ever need.

Your Father is full of grace for every moment of your life; He never runs out. Your brokenness is not too much for him, and your weakness does not disturb him. In his heart of love, there is everything you need for healing. He has already made accessible to you every tool you need to succeed, for he is the source of all life. Come and be filled!

God of abundance, in you is all I am longing for and everything I need. Fill me up with your grace that empowers me to live connected to you. I need you more than I know how to express. Meet me with your unfailing love today.

Unseen

We don't focus our attention on what is seen but on what is unseen.
For what is seen is temporary, but the unseen realm is eternal.
2 CORINTHIANS 4:18 TPT

What we focus our attention on matters. God's kingdom is full of the treasures found in his unfailing love. When we spend our time caught up in the changing circumstances of our lives without grounding ourselves in the reality of eternity, it can be overwhelming.

When we shift our awareness to God's character, we are looking with eyes that see the promise of his kingdom come because he is faithful to do all he said he would. Let us fix our eyes on God, the author and perfecter of our faith. He never wavers in kindness, and his compassion never ends. They are as eternal as God himself. When we look for evidence of his goodness, we will surely find it.

Lord, help me to fix my eyes on you and on eternity rather than on the momentary troubles around me. Give me your perspective, so I may see the way you do. Fill my thoughts with yours, Lord, and make me more like you.

Rest

*"Come to me, all you who are weary and burdened,
and I will give you rest."*

MATTHEW 11:28 NIV

When you find yourself overextended and exhausted, what do you do? Do the worries of life spill over from one day to the next, adding layer upon layer until you feel like you can't take another step? Jesus invites you to come to him and lay down your heavy burdens. He is able to give you the rest that you long for as he does all the heavy lifting.

Don't hesitate to approach him with all you have; he is waiting with open arms. He is full of kindness, not a lecture that you're dreading. Let his gentleness surprise you as you offer him your heaviness and he fills you with light and life! Come and find rest in him today.

Kind Father, I come to you today with all the heaviness I've been carrying. I can't keep going on this way. Lift my burdens and fill me with the peace that gives true rest to my soul. I need you.

Strength for Today

My life's strength melts away with grief and sadness;
come strengthen me and encourage me with your words.

PSALM 119:28 TPT

Sometimes the stresses of life, even the small, mundane, and ordinary things, feel like too much to face. Have you been relying on your own motivation to get through the recent days and weeks? Or has sadness stripped away any desire to do anything outside of what's necessary?

God is faithful to give us strength in our weakness—every single one. There is not a day where we are left on our own to figure things out. His grace is always available to empower and strengthen us, though that may not look like getting done everything we'd hoped. His strength carries us. When we are stripped of the enthusiasm we once had for life, we must adjust our expectations of what strength looks like. What would personal and profound encouragement from the Lord look like for you today?

Holy One, you are the strength that carries me through my darkest days. I won't worry about what tomorrow will bring; today, I fix my eyes on you. Come strengthen and encourage me like only you can.

Hopeful Expectation

The helpless has hope,
and unrighteousness must shut its mouth.
JOB 5:16 NASB

As children are completely dependent on their parents to provide what they cannot, so are we dependent on God. For some of us, it is harder to lean into our needs. When we find ourselves out of our depths and overcome with helplessness, where do we turn? There are some circumstances that can't be fixed by anything we could even dream of offering.

Where is our hope then? Is it in our own strength and capabilities, or does it lie in the one who formed us and all things around us? The Creator's character is flawless and his faithfulness is unmatched. This limited life is not where the fulfillment of our expectation will be found though we have sweet glimpses of our eternal hope. There is coming a day where there will be no more tears or sadness, and the old will have passed away. Where does your confidence lie?

God over all, you are bigger than I can fathom. I'm so grateful that you see from a higher perspective than I do. I ask for your holy hope to fill my heart today with the confidence of your goodness. You are worthy!

Wait

For God alone, O my soul, wait in silence,
for my hope is from him.
PSALM 62:5 ESV

Sometimes waiting feels like sitting in a fluorescent-lit office, anticipating your name being called. Other times, it is more like fighting a battle, awaiting reinforcements to come refuel your waning resources and help turn the tide of the war. Whatever waiting looks like for you today, are you anticipating God's response?

There is so much strength and hope to be found in him no matter how long your wait ends up being. Yield your heart to him today, giving him space to speak his words of life. He delights over you with songs of deliverance. You will not be disappointed in the way he pulls off redemption in your life.

God, I wait for you. When everything feels endless and barren, draw near and fill me with the fruit of your presence that never dissatisfies. You are so good; I cling to that reminder today. I quiet my heart before you now. Come and speak to me again.

Enough

*"That is why I tell you not to worry about everyday life—
whether you have enough food to eat or enough clothes to wear."*
LUKE 12:22 NLT

Have you ever taken inventory of the worries that fill your mind? How many of them are based on what will happen today? The thing about worry is that it is often caught up in what-ifs and scenarios that may or may not ever happen. Often they are based in the future, and much of it far off.

Jesus, when speaking to his disciples, said that we should not worry about everyday life. We will have what we need when we need it. There is always enough. What have you been worrying about that is simply draining your energy? Can you trust God today to provide for everything you need? He is always on time. Think through your life. Have there been times when you were worried about something and it ended up working out? Thank God for his faithfulness. He hasn't changed.

Father, I can see how you have provided for me before, and I believe that you will do it again. I trust that you are sufficient for me and that you're never late. Fill my thoughts with your goodness.

Cast off Troubles

Banish anxiety from your heart
and cast off the troubles of your body,
for youth and vigor are meaningless.

ECCLESIASTES 11:10 NIV

There is no way to avoid troubles in this life. They come, as surely as the seasons change. Anxieties mount as we consider how ill-equipped we are to face the challenges. Our bodies react to the uncertainties we face. But this is not where our stories end. We are not destined to cycles of uncontrollable angst. The creator of our bodies, minds and souls is full of peace that he freely gives.

When was the last time you felt God's presence calm your anxious thoughts and bring peace to your hurried mind? The Spirit gives comfort and can fill you with the unfailing love of God that pushes fear aside. If you find yourself worried, ask the Lord to draw near in his presence. He is faithful to come.

Holy Spirit, come fill me with the power of your presence. Bring peace to my anxious heart and calm my hurried mind. I rely on you. I cannot do it on my own, and I'm so glad that I don't have to. You are welcome to have your way in me, Lord, for I belong to you.

goodness

*I would have despaired unless I had believed
that I would see the goodness of the LORD
in the land of the living.*

PSALM 27:13 NASB

We have such a great hope in what awaits us after this short life; yet, it doesn't feel like enough to only hope for what feels so incredibly intangible. We need to know goodness now. God is in the business of restoration! He deals in mending the wounded, binding up the brokenhearted, and bringing life out of dead things. He never gives up or throws his hands up declaring something out of his reach.

If it feels like the end for you, it is not. God always has a better plan. Plot twists come, but his faithfulness never wavers. When was the last time you saw the goodness of God show up tangibly in your life? Where there is disappointment in your heart, there is also an invitation for God's powerful presence to shift your perspective.

Good Father, I admit that I have felt the desperation of hard circumstances in my life. I have to believe that I will see your goodness again! Give me eyes to see that you are moving, even now, and tenacity to hold onto hope when it is difficult to decipher what you are doing.

Confident Help

We can say with confidence, "The LORD is my helper,
so I will have no fear. What can mere people do to me?"

There are some situations that are completely out of our control. We cannot dictate the outcomes, and it sometimes seems that whatever we try to do to help only intensifies the issues. What then should we do? We don't need to be in control to be at peace. God is our help in every single circumstance.

God cannot be confused or confounded. Your troubles are not too complex for him to handle. In his perfect wisdom, he always knows exactly what to do. Will you trust him to do what you can't? Will you relent your need to fix and let him be your help? He is more than capable in this, and every, situation.

Lord, you are my willing help in every hour of need. You never withdraw your presence, leaving me to figure things out on my own. I surrender my need to control and let you take the reins. You are always faithful. My confidence lies in you.

Humble Heart

God gives us even more grace, as the Scripture says,
"God is against the proud, but he gives grace to the humble."
JAMES 4:6 NCV

Failure is not a sin but an eventuality of humanity. It's ok to try and not succeed; it is not a character flaw to be imperfect. When we do make mistakes that affect both others and us in hurtful ways, there is so much grace. Not just enough grace but plentiful mercy that overflows!

When we humbly approach God, there is unfailing love that meets us every time. He doesn't sometimes encounter us with kindness and other times with harsh discipline. Even his correction is drenched in compassion. Let us not lose heart in approaching God at every opportunity. His tender heart is full of power to heal, refine, and liberate.

God, I come to you with a humble heart, longing for your tender mercy to meet me again. I cannot test the limits of your compassion. There are no boundaries to your love. I offer myself as your own again; fill me with the power of your presence that sets me free.

Joy for Mourning

Those who sow in tears
shall reap with shouts of joy.
PSALM 126:5 ESV

When we are overcome by sadness, the Comforter is close. There is no escaping pain in this life; it finds each one of us in time. Broken promises, the loss of loved ones, and dashed hopes are all situations that we face. Even so, God is not surprised, and he is not distant.

Jesus was acquainted with suffering and familiar with pain. He did not require his followers to deny the reality of their circumstances; rather, he offered them hope in healing, joy in restoration, and the incredible satisfaction of right relationship with God. Whatever sorrows we are facing now will pale in comparison to the joy that is coming!

Lord, I cannot deny the sadness of my heart in heartbreak and in despair. In your goodness, touch me with the liquid love of your presence. Comfort me and revive my weary heart. There is no one who can do it, but I know that you can. Give me perspective to see that this suffering is temporary but your joy is eternal.

Saved

"I, I am the Lord, and besides me there is no savior. I declared and saved and proclaimed, when there was no strange god among you; and you are my witnesses," declares the Lord, "and I am God.
Isaiah 43:11-12 esv

When the drudgery of life wears down our defenses and we are left feeling vulnerable and raw, what is our response? Do we just try harder? Do we hunker down and keep going, hoping that at some point things will change? Unless we have help, there is certainly little hope for transformation.

When our reserves are tapped, we can't be expected to thrive. However, God is the source of every good thing and he never runs out or runs dry. He is the help we need and the Savior that continually comes through for us. Where we feel overwhelmed and under fire from every side, may we call out to our faithful God who rescues us.

Faithful One, I depend on you for help in every trouble I face. I cannot save myself. You know how I've tried! Don't stop showing off in power, and please don't ever stop reaching out in mercy. I am yours. Fill my heart with the confidence of your closeness.

Tired

I'm exhausted! My life is spent with sorrow,
my years with sighing and sadness.
Because of all these troubles,
I have no more strength.
My inner being is so weak and frail.

PSALM 31:10 TPT

God does not shy away from the reality of our lives or neglect the weariness that can erode our hope. He is not afraid of our big emotions, and he doesn't require us to get it all together before we come to him. In fact, he is the source where we will find the refreshing we are so desperate for.

Are you tired? Is sadness a constant companion these days? God does not promise us a pain-free existence, but he does vow to comfort us and empower us to life. Where your strength is depleted, invite the presence of God to cover you with his love. He will not fail to meet you with the power of his nearness. His love is better than anything else you can taste or experience in this world. May his compassion be your comfort and your deepest delight.

Merciful God, meet me in my weakness and empower me with your Spirit. You refresh me when I am completely depleted. Do it again, Lord.

Fulfilled Hope

Oh that I might have my request,
and that God would fulfill my hope.

JOB 6:8 ESV

How are your levels of hope these days? Do you have confident expectation of God's faithful witness in your life or are you struggling to believe that you will see his goodness at all? There is no wrong answer; God's faithfulness is not dependent on your faith. He is constant and unchanging, no matter what is or isn't a present reality in your life.

May your heart take courage in the loyalty of God to his own Word. He has not failed his children, and he won't fail you. Though troubles and trials come, the promise of the Lord is not thrown off track. God is the fulfiller of dreams. Submit your heart to him again, whether you are full of hope or desperately hanging on to a thread of it. He will prove true to you. His tender mercy is yours in every moment.

Good God, even when I struggle to hope, you remain constant. What a relief that I can't talk you out of your faithfulness. I give you access to my heart again, and ask that you would breathe peace, hope, and love into my being. As I wait on you, I will find strength. You meet me in the middle of every moment.

Trust

Preserve me, O God,
for in you I put my trust.
PSALM 16:1 NKJV

What does active trust look like? Is it blind hope that keeps its fingers crossed throughout the hard times? Is it a continual surrender of our own control and belief that God will stay true to his nature? It is so much more than a one-time statement of faith. As we practice placing our hope in God over and over again, our confidence will grow as he continues to show up in faithfulness.

God is a refuge to those who seek shelter in his name. He preserves and keeps us safe in his mercy. What he gives no one and nothing can take away: no storm, no evil person, no hateful act, no betrayal. He is dependable in compassion and reliable in love!

Father, I continually put my trust in you. You know my heart and how it fluctuates, but I am grateful that you never change even when I do. Meet me with your loyal love and fill me with everything I need for today.

Radiant Hope

The Lord alone is our radiant hope
and we trust in him with all our hearts.
His wrap-around presence will strengthen us.
PSALM 33:22 TPT

When nothing seems to be going right, and we are overwhelmed by all that needs to be done, it can be hard to not spiral in worry. But God is our sure help in every season. When we rely on our own limited strategies to get us through, they will only take us so far. God's wisdom is better, and it is the perfect solution to every problem we encounter.

In our weakness, God meets us with the power of his presence and strengthens us. His Spirit wraps around us with the warmth of his love that embraces us. We find our hope in this place. He is the sweetest treasure in this life. His goodness is ever increasing. We have not seen the end of it. Let us trust him with all our hearts.

Lord, fill my heart with hope as I look to you. You surround me with your presence and my heart comes alive. I want to know you more today. Encourage my soul in the way that only you can.

Words of Hope

I rise before dawn and cry for help;
I put my hope in your words.
PSALM 119:147 NRSV

In the restlessness of endless thoughts that won't quit, worry sometimes leads to sleepless nights. When we cannot calm our minds, we have access to the giver of all peace. His presence is pure love; he comforts us in the middle of our mess, whether in the dark of night or the light of day. He is always available.

Are you struggling to find peace? Look into God's Word and you will find hope in his faithful character. He never fails, and he won't start now. Cry out for help and listen for his reply. He will answer you. He is not silent. When it is hard to hear, look for the mercy and kindness you may be resisting. It is clearly laid out in his Word. Seek and you'll find it.

God, you are my hope. I rely solely on you for the help I need. Come into the craziness of my circumstances and calm every fear with the faithful way you work. I trust that you have not left me alone. You are with me in the joys and the sorrows. Turn around what looks impossible and mark my life with your goodness.

One Thing

I have not achieved it,
but I focus on this one thing:
Forgetting the past
and looking forward to what lies ahead.

PHILIPPIANS 3:13 NLT

We have not reached the end of our hope. As long as we draw breath into our lungs, our story is not finished. When we get caught up in the shame of our past and can't see a way to move forward, we may struggle to believe that God's redemptive power can make our futures better. But that is simply not the truth.

What is your focus right now? Is it to be amazing at your job or to focus on being present with your family? Is it to get a degree? Maybe it's something much smaller. These are all great pursuits, though they are limited in their scope. With God as your main goal, knowing that his kingdom will come and his will be done on earth as it is in heaven, your hopes will be fulfilled.

Jesus, you are the one that I am running after in this life. Even as I run, I realize that through your presence in the Spirit, you are with me. I look to you for everything I need: I'm desperate for you to turn around what I have made a mess of. Come do what only you can do.

February

Why am I so sad?
Why am I so upset?
I should put my hope in God
and keep praising him.

PSALM 42:11 NCV

Loved

*Cast all your anxiety on him
because he cares for you.*
1 PETER 5:7 NRSV

When was the last time you shared the struggles you are experiencing in a real way? Certainly there is a difference between sharing your troubles with someone you barely know and sharing them with a trusted friend. When you think of giving your concerns to the Lord, which category does he fall into?

There is safety in the relationships where you know you are loved; you don't question the other's intentions toward you. God's love and care for you is greater than the expanse of the universe. You cannot reach the end because there is none. Are you willing to give your worries to the one who loves you better than anyone else can?

Loving Father, I give you my anxiety today. I don't want to carry it on my own any longer. Wrap me in your great love that casts out every fear and cover me with your peace that transcends my understanding.

Supported

"Don't worry, because I am with you.
Don't be afraid, because I am your God.
I will make you strong and will help you;
I will support you with my right hand that saves you."

ISAIAH 41:10 NCV

In our weakness, it is wise to lean on the support God provides. It is not failure to be helped; it is the reinforcement that causes us to be strengthened. When we think through those who have exhibited great faith, it isn't that they did great things on their own. That has never been the plot.

Abraham, Moses, Daniel, and Mary are a few examples of those who lived with perseverance. They also lived out incredible supernatural experiences, none of which were based on their own abilities. What are you facing right now that seems impossible? Is it as impossible as being thrown into a lion's den, or leaving for an unknown destination, or leading a nation of people into a desert? Be encouraged today that your fear can turn to faith with God's mighty strength supporting you.

Almighty God, I so often lose sight of your incredible faithfulness to those who call on you. I am yours, and I believe that even if I can't see how you will turn my circumstances around, you are with me every step of the way.

Here Now

"Do not worry about tomorrow;
for tomorrow will care for itself.
Each day has enough trouble of its own."
MATTHEW 6:34 NASB

The flowers of the field do not work and yet they bloom in beauty. The birds of the air are not responsible to produce their own food, and still God provides everything they need. How much more will God provide everything you need today?

When was the last time you let go of the unknowns that produce worry over your life? Try releasing them to God today and see what you are left with. Today is a fresh opportunity to embrace what is in front of you. What is yours to do? Who can you love? Leave tomorrow in God's hands and embrace the present. See how it changes your perspective.

Lord, I am grateful to know that you are not far off in the future. You are always present in every moment. I let go of the worries I've been carrying around and trust that as you always have so you will continue to provide for me and those I love.

Trust Jesus

"Don't worry or surrender to your fear.
For you've believed in God,
now trust and believe in me also."

JOHN 14:1 TPT

As the Son of God, Jesus reflects God the Father to the world. He is the tangible representation of love. Perfect love, as it says in first John, that drives out fear. Jesus laid down his very life to reveal the length that God would go for us to be reunited with him in love.

Where there is fear that threatens to overshadow the goodness in your life, there is an invitation to trust and believe in the one who knows no limitations. Let him love you to life again and again if that's what it takes. His grace is not transactional; it is not dependent on what you have to offer. Will you receive grace to believe in his goodness toward you today?

Great God, I don't want to be overrun by fear anymore. Where worry and dread have closed me in, I ask for your grace to tear down the walls and bring freedom. I trust you, Jesus, to surprise me with your love again.

Call Out

From the depths of despair, O LORD,
I call for your help.
PSALM 130:1 NLT

When anxiety builds like a pressure-cooker as thoughts race around your mind, desperation can take over. In the spiral, when it feels like everything is out-of-control, what do you do?

Calling out for help is sometimes all we have. When we have exhausted our own resources, we must rely on others. God is our ultimate help. When we feel isolated and alone, he is with us, ready with a Father's help. Thankfully, he has also created us for community. We were not meant to simply survive life on our own; we were always meant to be part of a family. Wherever we find ourselves in the present moment, we can know that help is within reach.

Jehovah, you are the keeper of all my days. When I come to the end of myself, I find that you have always been more than enough. Help me today in my desperation. I cannot save myself.

Strong Love

The LORD is my light and my salvation—
whom shall I fear?
The LORD is the stronghold of my life—
of whom shall I be afraid?

PSALM 27:1 NIV

In the storms of life, God's truth shines like a lighthouse, beckoning us to the safety of his love. He is like a fortified castle where we can take shelter and receive protection from the attack of the enemy. He is stronger than any weapon both formed and imagined. His love is strong enough to keep us safe.

When fear threatens to cripple you and it sends your mind spinning, where do you turn? Find refuge in the covering of your Father's love. Let him fight your battles for you; take rest in him. Let him be the foundation that grounds you. Will you let his perfect love cover you today, calming your anxieties and feelings of distress?

Loving God, I ask for your powerful love to calm all my anxious thoughts today. You are the shelter where I hide. I have no strength to fight, Lord. Be my defender!

Unashamed

*Hope does not put us to shame,
because God's love has been poured into our hearts
through the Holy Spirit who has been given to us.*

ROMANS 5:5 ESV

When things don't go our way, or we end up in situations that highlight our shortcomings, discouragement can easily set in. Disappointment turns to shame when we see these things attached to our worth. "I failed" becomes "I'm a failure." Though we inevitably fall short in life time and again, it does not mean that we are defined by failure.

Our true worth is found in whose we are. As children of God, we bear the resemblance of a good Father. No person is worthless. Not one. We are image bearers, continually loved to life by the source of all that is good and true. The Holy Spirit is our present help in times of trouble, and he never ever leaves us.

Ever-present One, pour your love into me again today with the sweetness of your presence. Remove all the residue of shame that has turned scars into character flaws; lift the weight of discouragement and fill me with hope again.

Safe and Secure

You will have confidence,
because there is hope;
you will be protected
and take your rest in safety.
JOB 11:18 NRSV

Children in healthy families are confident of their parents' ability to keep them safe and secure. Small children are not required to fend for themselves or to keep their environment safe; Mom and Dad take care of everything they need. Loving parents protect their families and their kids take comfort in the leadership they provide.

As children of God, we can rest in the knowledge that we are being cared for, provided for, and protected. We are not left on our own to figure things out. Our confidence is in our ever-present God who doesn't miss a detail. We can yield the unknown to him, trusting that he sees and provides for all we need.

Faithful Father, I trust that you will continue to take care of me as you have up until now. You are not absent. I have confidence in your goodness and I can rest in you, knowing that you don't miss a thing.

Words of Promise

Remember the word to Your servant,
Upon which You have caused me to hope.
PSALM 119:49 NKJV

God's Word is full of examples of his faithfulness. He is a keeper of promises. He doesn't change his mind. He speaks and then he acts (though often not in our timeline). All God's promises can be counted on because they depend on his own character. In him, all prophecies are fulfilled.

We can be grateful that God's promises, which bring us hope, are tied to the truth that exists in who he is. God is not a liar nor can he become one. May our hearts be encouraged today in the knowledge that he is a keeper of his word, and it is in his Word that we hope.

God of truth, I take hope in the knowledge that your word is sincere. You are faithful and true, and I trust in you. Where I have been disappointed, let my heart be encouraged in seeing you come through in better ways than I could have ever expected.

Keep Praying

*One day Jesus taught the apostles to keep praying
and never stop or lose hope.*
LUKE 18:1 TPT

When we call out to God, we are teaching our hearts to turn to him. As we continually pray and communicate with him, we can't help but be changed by the awareness that God is bigger than our present circumstances. He is bigger than our small lives can contain.

Jesus taught his disciples to pray, not just as something to do, but because it was how Jesus himself communicated with the Father. Jesus' life is a beautiful example of how to stay connected with God no matter what situations we may face. As Jesus lived, so should we—with hopeful expectation before us. Don't stop praying. The Father is always accessible.

Father, let love be the fuel to my life. When I am discouraged, help me to keep looking to you. I won't stop praying. Fill me with your hope again today.

Whole Heart

A happy heart is like good medicine,
but a broken spirit drains your strength.
PROVERBS 17:22 NCV

God binds up the brokenhearted. He takes what seems irreparable and makes it completely new. Where you are broken and hurting, invite the Lord to minister to you with the life of his presence. He brings what wasn't into being; he will not let you be crushed.

Today is the day of your healing. He has not forgotten you. As you give him access to your life, he takes the broken pieces and makes you whole. Find your hope in him. Where your strength has been depleted, he is coming to fill you up with his immeasurable grace that empowers you to thrive and not just survive. Lift your eyes to him.

Lord, where I have been struggling to just get through, come in and breathe new life that revives my soul. I have no hope apart from you. You are everything. With expectation, I invite you to do what only you can do: make my heart whole in your love. Nothing else will do.

Steady Ground

Every valley shall be raised up,
every mountain and hill made low;
the rough ground shall become level,
the rugged places a plain.

ISAIAH 40:4 NIV

There are many peaks and valleys as we walk through life. When we expect a continually smooth road, somewhere along the way our hope will be disappointed. Our God is faithful to be the firm foundation of our lives. He never changes. When everything that can be shaken in our lives is shaken, we find that we are still standing on God our rock.

When our hope is in God and not the details of our lives, we find the courage we need to trust him no matter what is going on. One day there will be no more need for faith in what we cannot see because everything that is hidden will be made clear. Until that day, let us keep trusting in our God who never wavers.

Faithful One, my heart takes hope in the reality that you never change. You are my strength when I am weak, my shelter in the storms of life, and my joy in the middle of suffering. Lead me on in your love, Lord, and bring me into freedom so that even when I am walking through the valley, I am full of your presence.

Joyful Surrender

Taste and see that the LORD is good.
Oh, the joys of those who take refuge in him!
PSALM 34:8 NLT

When was the last time you were overcome with the joy of knowing God and his goodness? Have you felt the freedom that his affection over you brings? Take refuge in him today and let him take care of what you cannot. The fruit of his kingdom is that which brings life to your soul: it is love, joy, peace, and kindness.

Today is the perfect opportunity to lay down your burdens at the feet of your God and King. Let him do the heavy lifting; as you rest in him, you will find the restoration your weary soul has been longing for. Taste and see that the Lord is good!

Good God, you are my safe place of refuge. I bring you every worry, care, and burden that has been weighing me down. I lay them at your feet today. As I exchange my heavy burdens for your light ones, I am able to breathe deeply again. What a relief! You are my freedom and my joy.

Higher Love

Your lovingkindness, O Lord,
extends to the heavens,
Your faithfulness reaches to the skies.
PSALM 36:5 NASB

There is no limit to the love of God. It is so much sweeter, so much better, than any love we could experience this side of heaven. His intentions are pure. His heart toward us is full of fiery love that does not belittle or make us feel less than anyone or anything. His love lifts the lonely; it is extravagantly poured out at every opportunity.

God cannot be understood apart from his deep affection because his very nature is love. He is not a dictator, requiring us to fall in line because he said so. He loves us to life at every turn with kindness and gentleness. Even his correction is laced with love. His love is abundantly available to us in every moment, including right now.

Loving God, give me a fresh revelation of the depth of your affection today. Where it has felt stale, breathe new insight into the depths of my heart, opening my eyes to the greatness of your love. You are better than I expect at every turn. Thank you for your great mercy that covers me all the days of my life.

Dependable

The word of the LORD is upright,
and all his work is done in faithfulness.
PSALM 33:4 ESV

Many of us grow up in families where we learn to depend on ourselves for our needs. Even those of us from stable families may have found that we coped with various circumstances by withdrawing and seeking solutions where needs were left unmet. This was never the model we were meant to live.

God is a good Father. He is always available and he meets every need. He is dependable and trustworthy. You don't need to figure things out on your own; you don't need to suffer through the consequences of your circumstances in isolation. You were created to lean on your Father's help. You can never outgrow your status as a child of the living God. Take the opportunity that today provides to ask for help when you need it; he lovingly intervenes for your benefit.

Lord, I humbly offer you my heart today. See where I fall short; I so easily do! I need your help, God, and I don't want to keep striving in my own strength. You always know better than I do. I lean into your loyal love today, knowing I will receive help whenever I need it.

Protected

The Lord is faithful, who will establish you
and guard you from the evil one.
2 THESSALONIANS 3:3 NKJV

When you feel lost to your circumstances, nearly drowning in the worries of this world, there is a place of refuge available. God, your rescuer, will not let you be crushed by your situation. He is faithful to save you every single time. He is your protector and the guardian of your soul. Let every lie that stands between you and the freedom of God's intentions toward you come crashing down today.

You have been found by a faithful Father, and he never hesitates in his affections for you. The love of the father of the prodigal son is just a glimpse into the goodness of God toward his children. Where you have wondered about your worth, let the love of God wash over you in abundance. He will always pick you up and welcome you into his warm embrace with joy.

Faithful One, you are the one I lean on. I depend on you to guard and protect me from the evil one. Love of God, flood my mind, my heart, and my body today. I receive the kindness of your heart. I am yours. May I forever be found in you.

Firmly Planted

To all who mourn in Israel,
he will give a crown of beauty for ashes,
a joyous blessing instead of mourning,
festive praise instead of despair.
In their righteousness, they will be like great oaks
that the Lord has planted for his own glory.

ISAIAH 61:3 NLT

God is close to those who mourn. He meets us in the middle of our sorrow. But he doesn't stop there. He promises to give us beauty for ashes, joy instead of mourning, celebratory praise instead of despair. We are firmly planted in the love of the Lord.

Do not despair in your mourning. You don't need to pretend that things are better than they are. You don't need to will yourself to be positive. God is your source. He is the initiator of this great exchange. He will not leave you on your own, and you will not be lost to the anguish of your soul. He has planted you in his kingdom, and he will tend to you.

Merciful God, I am so thankful for your presence that never leaves. I trust that you are right here with me in every moment. Increase my awareness of your closeness. Cover me with your love and lift my head to see your goodness today.

Keep Asking

Do not worry about anything,
but pray and ask God for everything you need,
always giving thanks.

PHILIPPIANS 4:6 NCV

God does not weary of your questions or your wonderings. Like a patient father, he welcomes your musings and your quirky thoughts at every opportunity. He is not ambivalent toward you. He delights in your asking. He never turns away from an open heart no matter what is spilling out.

Let today be the day you don't censor yourself with God. Ask him for everything you need. Don't hold back your doubts. He can handle them, and you don't need to keep them bottled up. With the gratefulness of a heart that is openly received, don't stop yourself from airing out the corners of your mind with him. How he delights in communion with you!

Provider, I will not hesitate to freely come to you with everything on my mind today. I am so thankful that your heart is open and your ears are attentive to me. I will not stop myself from asking and seeking for fear that you will grow tired of me. I will train my mind to be freely open with you today. Thank you, Lord!

Wasted Energy

*"Can any one of you by worrying
add a single hour to your life?"*

MATTHEW 6:27 NIV

When life gets overwhelming, what do you do? Does your mind run away with all the possibilities of what could happen? When you don't know how something will turn out, it can be second nature to worry about it. As Jesus questioned, though, how often does worry add anything to your life?

God is all-seeing and all-knowing. It is not wishful thinking to trust him to guide us through every hill and valley. Where confusion clouds our understanding, God is completely confident. Lean on him and his wisdom today. He won't let his children down.

Great God, I am so grateful that you are not confused by anything. I remind myself that you are above it all. I trust you today: I align myself with your truth and your wisdom. I'm leaning on you. When I am tempted to worry, I will turn that energy toward trusting you.

Able

Can any idols of the nations bring rain?
Or can the heavens give showers?
Is it not you, O LORD our God?
We set our hope on you,
for it is you who do all this.
JEREMIAH 14:22 NRSV

God is able to do all that we could ever think or imagine and so much more! He is the hope that holds us together when everything around us is falling apart. He is the source of every good thing. He never stops working, never pauses his plans, and he does not grow weary of faithfully showing up in love.

What would it look like to align ourselves in complete and total trust to our Maker? What would happen if we gave ourselves fully to believing that he would come through just like he said he would? His track record is impeccable. He does not fail. Let our hope be firmly planted in the heart of our faithful God.

Lord of heaven and earth, who is there like you? You are faithful beyond all measure. Who can count the ways that you reveal your lovingkindness to your people? Show up again in power, Lord. I put all my hope and trust in you!

all I Need

"The Lord is my portion," says my soul,
"therefore I will hope in him."
LAMENTATIONS 3:24 ESV

There is no need we have that is met outside of God's grace. He is the portion we crave, and he is so satisfying. Where we see the unmet desires of our heart, there is space for God's provision. He does not delight in our anxiety, nor does he take satisfaction in our disappointment.

God's heart is full of abundance for every longing we have. He is the giver of good gifts and the fulfillment of the joy we crave. May we find our hearts' desires met in his fullness. As those who have gone before us, let us put our hope in him, for surely he will not let us down.

Lord, you are my portion. Everything I need is found in you, and I come with expectation today to receive out of the fullness of your heart. I rely on you. You alone are my confidence.

Deliverance Is Coming

*"Keep your hope to the end
and you will experience life and deliverance."*
MATTHEW 24:13 TPT

In the waiting, it can be hard not to grow discouraged. This is where our attention matters. What are we surrounding ourselves with? Do we fellowship with others who help us and lift us up, or do we plug along with the disheartened and discouraged? There is a place for sharing in suffering, and it should not be underrated. The messages we receive from media, faithless friends, and society at large, affect us.

What are our souls being fed with? Is it the despair of the world or is it the hope of the kingdom? We cannot escape the harsh realities of life, but we certainly can take ownership of the messages we allow into our homes and hearts. God is our hope, and he is our deliverer! May we choose to align ourselves with the love of Jesus, displayed in the Word and in fellowship with others who are submitted to his grace.

God, as I cling to your Word, I know that life and deliverance are coming. Even as I wait on you, I choose to continue to believe in hope that you are coming and you will restore all that has been lost. You are consistently good, and I choose to trust in your goodness.

Shared Comfort

Our hope for you is firmly grounded,
knowing that as you are sharers of our sufferings,
so also you are sharers of our comfort.

2 CORINTHIANS 1:7 NASB

There is encouragement in the experience of sharing in another's burdens. When we don't have to carry a heavy load alone, we are filled with courage and strength to keep going. We are not meant to bear our heaviness alone. This was never a part of God's design. He created us for fellowship.

When God created Adam, he did not stop there. He declared that it was not good for man to be alone, so he made a companion in Eve. This was the blueprint at the beginning, and it is still the standard. We were made for relationship—for family. As we share in each other's sufferings, so do we share in comfort.

Father, I see you in the beauty of community. Your Word says that you set the lonely in families. Where I have been alone and isolated, I ask that you would give me the fellowship I crave. Your heart is shown clearly in relationship; it's what I was made for. Thank you for your comfort in people around me. Help me to stay connected!

Sincere Hope

We desire each one of you to show the same earnestness
to have the full assurance of hope until the end.
HEBREWS 6:11 ESV

When our hope is in God, it is not frivolous or wishful thinking. The same God who raises the dead to life is the God who will complete the work he began in us. Belief in God is not a fad, nor does it prove to be unfruitful. When the going gets tough, do we continue to turn our eyes to Jesus and press into his faithful love, or do we walk away in disappointment?

Let your heart be encouraged that the hope you have is not based on the happiness you may or may not feel in the moment. In the darkest night, God is with you. He is steadfast and secure, never failing. Don't be tricked into thinking that if you don't feel good about how your life is going, then you must not be cut out for faith. Let your confidence be found in God's steady nature!

Faithful One, I set my thoughts on your character today. May my heart be full of courage to keep believing and trusting that you will never fail. I rely on you and on your love.

Hold On

Let us hold fast the confession of our hope without wavering,
for He who promised is faithful.

HEBREWS 10:23 NASB

The nature of God is far beyond any good character that we could exhibit in our lives. His faithfulness never fails. Not once. His loyal love never hesitates. It is always flowing, never receding. There is no need for him to ask for forgiveness because he is perfect in all his ways: the ways we understand and those we don't.

Let us not be foolish enough to think that we know better than God. At the same time, let's ascribe to him what belongs to him—the praise and gratefulness he deserves. As we do, our hearts are turned to him in adoration. Not everything that happens to us in life is from God. Let us remember that there is an enemy that seeks to steal, kill, and destroy. May we hold fast to our hope in the King of love who never betrays his character.

God over all, I have seen your faithfulness in my life: even now as I look, I see it! May my heart be bound to yours in love that all my days I would stay tucked into your mercy, clinging to who you are. Thank you for relationship with you: you are beautiful in all your ways!

Patient Endurance

You also keep your hopes high and be patient,
for the presence of the Lord is drawing closer.
JAMES 5:8 TPT

Just as a farmer waits patiently for his harvest, knowing that nature needs to run its course, so we should remember that we are waiting for a coming King who will appear in the proper time. The farmer does what he knows to do, but he cannot speed up the harvest.

In the same way, our hopes are set on a promise that will be fulfilled through Christ's return. Though the waiting is long, to our standards, the time is coming. As we linger in the in-between space, we do what we are called to do, all the while being confident that the harvest is sure to come. Even as we wait, we have the very presence of God with us who fills us with courage, joy, peace, and the abundance of his love.

Yahweh, you are the God who was, who is, and who always will be. I have placed all my bets on you; let my heart be convinced of your goodness and faithfulness. Holy Spirit, fill me with the love that fuels my freedom. You are my joy and my great reward!

Mindful Discipline

Prepare your minds for action; discipline yourselves; set all your hope on the grace that Jesus Christ will bring you when he is revealed.
1 PETER 1:13 NRSV

Living by faith is not circumstantial, and it is not produced by accident. Faith is an active choosing to believe in something or someone. In the world of spirituality, discipline can get a bad rap. However, when we look into the practice of spiritual disciplines, they benefit our faith by training us to align to God's kingdom ways.

Have you been floating along in your faith, or have you been able to regulate your mind and actions in partnership with the Spirit? There is no condemnation or judgment for where you are at today. Take hope in the grace that God freely gives to empower you to live liberated in his law of love. If you don't know where to begin, start by directing your heart toward him through his Word and through prayer.

Holy One, you freely give to all those who ask for help in your name. Fill me with your grace that gives me the strength to live aligned with your life and light. May the boundaries of my heart be expanded, even as I actively restrict where my attentions go. You are worthy of my obedience!

Don't Give Up

Though He slay me, I will hope in Him.
Nevertheless I will argue my ways before Him.

JOB 13:15 NASB

When life's circumstances are grim and confusing, it is hard not to believe that even God is against us. But that is not his nature. He is a wrap-around shield to those who take refuge in him. Though our situations don't always line up with God's character, his presence fills us with what we need—even in the face of tragedy and sorrow.

Will we continue to hope in God when everything seems to be falling apart in our lives? As we struggle to sense his goodness with us, will we dare to cling to him even then? Will we risk depending on God even when those around us give up? If the mountains fall into the sea and the nations rage against each other, God is still the same merciful, all-powerful God he always was.

Merciful Father, I bind my heart to yours in hope today. Give me confidence as I walk in your way of love. Even as I press on, I ask that you would give me the tenacity to hold onto you no matter what. I believe, Lord, help my unbelief!

March

You, O Lord, are a shield about me,

my glory, and the lifter of my head.

PSALM 3:3 ESV

Fulfillment

He will not ignore forever all the needs of the poor,
for those in need shall not always be crushed.
Their hopes shall be fulfilled, for God sees it all!

PSALM 9:18 TPT

The God of all creation, full of both power and kindness, will not turn a blind eye to those who are in need. When we feel alone in our struggle, we can find rest in the one who sees it all. We will not be crushed by these momentary troubles that burden us.

When was the last time you felt hope for your life? Today, take a moment to recall God's faithfulness in your life. When you felt overwhelmed by fear and overcome by worry in the past, did marinating in those feelings help you? Some days feel like too much to bear. Will you invite God's presence to breathe hope into you again and shake off the dust of the pressures that are beyond you?

Powerful One, I trust in your Word that says I am not alone in my struggles. You see everything, and I am known by you. Remind me again of your faithfulness and encourage my heart to hope in you.

good god

The Lord is good to those whose hope is in him,
to the one who seeks him.

LAMENTATIONS 3:25 NIV

We can find hope when we press into the goodness of God. Some days, and even some seasons, this can be a difficult practice. When circumstances are confusing and cycles of shame seem unending, we can forget what God's goodness tastes like.

Are you waiting until you feel better to seek the Lord? Have you been hiding from him, or ignoring the pull of his presence because you're upset with him? There is nothing that is too much for the Lord. Not your doubts, worries, anger, or fear. Bring them to him today and taste the kindness of one who leads in love; he will not condemn your heart that seeks truth.

Father, I come to you today with all that I've been holding back. I cannot hide the state of my heart from you, and I don't want to. Here I am, Lord. Here is all I have. Speak your better word over my life today. I need to hear from your heart.

Morning Is Coming

That time of darkness and despair
will not go on forever.

ISAIAH 9:1 NLT

In life, there are inevitable dark nights of the soul. Grief is unavoidable; we are all acquainted with loss. The deep sorrow that fills us when we mourn both great and seemingly invisible losses is not something that we can wish ourselves out of. Jesus knew this well as the Man of Sorrows. He is familiar with suffering and anguish. We do not need to hide this part of ourselves from him.

Knowing that he sees and knows it all through eyes of love, how will you approach him with your broken heart? Will you trust him to care for you, and even carry you, through the times when you have nothing to offer?

Ever-present One, I have to believe that when the sun rises on my dark night, I will see evidence of your goodness that was with me all along. I offer you myself though it's not much. I am grateful that you love me for me and not for what I can do for you. Hold me near, Lord. I need you.

Fed by Love

He has brought me to his banquet hall,
And his banner over me is love.

SONG OF SOLOMON 2:4 NASB

God has prepared a place for you at his banqueting table. You are not welcomed in as a stranger but as a friend. Your place will not be filled by another—it is yours alone. See how the Father welcomes you with affection today. Come as you are and feast on his love.

You don't have to clean yourself up to come before him. God will rain over you with his lovingkindness and lighten your load with his warm embrace. His refreshing presence will assure you of the delight you bring him. When was the last time you felt loved and accepted just as you are?

Loving Father, I want to know your thoughts toward me today. Help me to see what you see without the shame and worthlessness that has been clouding my thoughts. Your love is strong enough to hold every part of my world; help me to let go of control and trust that you really are all I need.

Spirit Fruit

*God will never give you the spirit of fear,
but the Holy Spirit who gives you
mighty power, love, and self-control.*

1 TIMOTHY 1:7 TPT

What a wonderful gift we've been given in the Holy Spirit who fills us, guides us, and empowers us to live as Christ did. We can know that when we are filled with fear that immobilizes us, it is not from the Lord. Rather, the Spirit of God is full of love, grace, strength, and peace.

When the frenzy of fear has us feeling like we need to make hasty decisions in order to right what is off kilter in our lives, it is an opportunity to slow down, take a breath, and gauge the source. God does not create anxiety in our hearts. He gives us peace that calms the storms within us. When was the last time you knew that kind of peace?

Holy Spirit, I am so grateful for your presence in my life. Even when I can't sense you, I know that you are with me. Fill me with your peace that calms my anxious thoughts and worried heart. Do what only you can do and change me from the inside out.

Confident Perseverance

Do not throw away your confidence,
which has a great reward.
HEBREWS 10:35 NCV

When winter comes, we find ourselves faced with a new rhythm. Nature shows us that there are cycles to life. In the slowdown of winter, when the days are shorter, we can rest assured that it won't last forever. When spring breaks and we see new life sprouting up everywhere, it is a reminder of the rebirth that comes out of every dark season.

Your dark, cold winter of the soul will also end and you will experience the rebirth of spring again. Whatever season you find yourself in at the moment, you can be confident that it won't last forever. Do not despair if your winter has felt long. New life is coming. It is on the way. You will see the goodness of your God in the land of the living.

Steady One, I lean into your wisdom today. I trust that I will see the beauty of new life springing, even if all I see now is barrenness. Uplift my heart today, God, with hope. Lighten the weight of unmet expectations as I lift my eyes to you.

Continue to Believe

These things I have written to you who believe in the name of the Son of God, that you may know that you have eternal life, and that you may continue to believe in the name of the Son of God.

1 JOHN 5:13 NKJV

If you have trusted in Jesus as your Savior and yielded your life to him, you can be sure that you will receive the fruit that living a life for him brings. The nearness of God in the Holy Spirit who comforts, guides, and heals is yours for all of your days. Do not give up hope when life takes a turn. Troubles come and go, but they are not the final word over your life.

As believers, our hope is not limited to this short time on earth—it is so much greater! We have eternal life with God waiting on the other side. May we press on believing that God is who he says he is. His faithfulness will never come to an end. We can rest in the assurance of our place in God's kingdom.

Son of God, in you is the fulfillment of every promise. Your love is constant and true, and it is persistently covering me all the days of my life. I choose to continue to believe in you. You are better than I can even comprehend. Thank you for your faithfulness.

Come Boldly

Let us come boldly to the throne of our gracious God.
There we will receive his mercy,
and we will find grace to help us
when we need it most.

HEBREWS 4:16 NLT

As children of God, we have access to his presence. When Jesus died and the veil inside the temple that kept the people from the holy of holies was torn, every hindrance that could keep us from him was removed. We can come shamelessly into the presence of our God and King, knowing that we will be met by his kindness.

There is nothing that can keep us from his love and mercy. Will we boldly enter his presence, bringing all that we are before him? There we will find the strength we need and the grace that empowers us to live out what we could never do on our own. Why would we try to fight our way into his good standing when we have free access just as we are?

Merciful One, I approach you confidently, knowing that I am welcome in whatever state I come. Meet me with your love, filling me with the grace I so desperately need. You are the source of everything I'm longing for. I need you. Thank you for always accepting me as I am. I belong to you.

Power to Stand

Be strong in the Lord and in his mighty power.
Put on the full armor of God,
so that you can take your stand against the devil's schemes.
EPHESIANS 6:10-11 NIV

When we are out of our depth, and we don't know how to move forward, we will quickly find that desperation leads to a sense of being overwhelmed. Even the best problem solvers in the world are limited by their scope of understanding. Thankfully, we are not expected to fight our battles in our own strength, relying on our limited resources.

In God's mighty power, we can find ultimate strength. He has given us instructions for life and for the battles that rage in teaching us to wear his armor. Clothed in faith, truth, holiness, the power of salvation, and the readiness of the gospel of peace, we will be covered for everything we face. We will find the power to stand our ground as we lean into the wisdom of the Lord.

Wise God, you have given me everything I need to thrive in life. I will not neglect your Word as I face the battles before me. I cannot fight in my own strength; if I did, I would be beaten down time and again. I rely on you, God. You are my strength and the light of my life.

Possibility

"All things are possible to him who believes."
MARK 9:23 NASB

When we are in a privileged place in life, things feel easy. Yet, even those who have ease will face inevitable struggles. When we are struggling to make it through the days, weeks, and months, it can be a battle to hope for better. Jesus faced the trials and struggles that we do, and yet he never wavered in faith.

Will we be found as people of faith like Abraham who waited for the promise of his son far longer than he expected? Will we press on in the face of what looks like barrenness? Will we trust the Word of God when it seems impossible like Mary did when the angel told her she was going to mother the Son of God? God's ways are mysterious, but his faithfulness is not a guessing game!

All powerful God, I want to be perseverant in faith even when everything in my life looks like it goes against your promises. Help me to cling to you, knowing that you are faithful to your Word every time. You have not changed who you are, and I can trust in your unfailing love to cover me every step of the journey of my life.

Living God

To this end we toil and strive,
because we have our hope set on the living God,
who is the Savior of all people,
especially of those who believe.

HEBREWS 6:11 ESV

God is the same yesterday, today, and forever. When we consider the works of his hands, the miracles he has displayed, the wonders of his glorious love, may our hearts be encouraged to press on in hope. He has not grown silent, and he has not stopped working. He is as alive today as he was when Jesus walked the earth. He is as faithful today as he was to Abraham and Moses.

His ways are mysterious to us because we only see and know in part. He sees all and knows all. He understands the whole picture and is intimately aware of the minute details. Our hearts can find courage as we trust his wisdom over our own. May we continue to walk in the power and love of our living God who is present with us in the middle of every moment!

Living God, you are incredibly patient and kind with me. I find myself wanting my heart to believe in confidence that you are who you say you are. Fill me with your presence that calms my anxious fears and stills my chaotic thoughts. You are my portion.

All I Have

I cried out to you, Lord, my only hiding place.
You're all I have, my only hope in this life,
my last chance for help.

PSALM 142:5 TPT

When situations are desperate and there are no clear answers before us, we are aware of our need for God to come through. When we've exhausted all our resources and we have nothing left to pull from, God's help is all we're left with. Though this may feel uncomfortable, his solutions are always best anyway.

Whether you find yourself in a dire circumstance or the mundane of your routine, you can be sure that God's help is always available to you. He is a shelter to those seeking respite from the storms of life. He is always ready to come to the aid of those who ask. Don't hesitate to cry out to him today.

Lord, you are my hiding place. I rely on your help to get me through every trial. I lean into your wisdom today. Fill me with the peace of your presence that passes all understanding.

Dawn Is Coming

My soul waits for the Lord
More than the watchmen for the morning;
Indeed, more than the watchmen for the morning.

PSALM 130:6 NASB

The darkness of night hides the beauty of the life growing all around us. There is a stillness that comes with the night, and clarity when we learn to depend on other senses. When we find ourselves unable to see and confused as to what is going on, we can learn to lean into the voice of our good God who promises to never leave us or abandon us.

The night never lasts forever; the sun always rises. So it is with the dark circumstances of life. They will not last forever. Dawn is coming. When the sun rises on this dark night of the soul, you will be able to see the life that was hidden from your sight. God's goodness has not forsaken you even in the blackest night. He promises to be with you until the end of the age. Where he is, there is life.

Faithful Friend, I take courage in your Word that promises that you won't ever leave me. I cling to the confident hope of the sun rising again, and I believe I will see your goodness in my life.

Planted

He will be strong, like a tree planted near water
that sends its roots by a stream.
It is not afraid when the days are hot;
its leaves are always green.
It does not worry in a year when no rain comes;
it always produces fruit.

JEREMIAH 17:8 NCV

The roots of our hearts are firmly planted by springs of living water. This living water flows with the love of our gracious God. Rooted here, life will always grow. Even when drought comes, we draw from a source that goes under the surface and nourishes our beings. Our hearts are continually fed by the compassion of God; such nutrients produce fruit that cannot be hidden.

When we find that there is not much to draw on in our lives nor circumstances for life and growth, we can be sure that everything we need is already provided. We are consistently nourished by the lifegiving presence of our God who is always near.

God, you are the source of every good and pure thing in my life. All the goodness that comes from my life has been created in the incubator of your love. May my heart continue to thrive in you even when dry seasons come. Thank you!

Joy in Comfort

When anxiety was great within me,
your consolation brought me joy.

PSALM 94:19 NIV

Thank the Lord that we are not left alone to be swept up by our sorrow and anxieties. In the middle of the chaos and confusion, the Spirit ministers to us with his peace and comfort. The presence of God is not an idea; it is the tangible experience of his nature. His comfort covers us like a blanket. His love fuels us like a stoked fire.

May our hearts be one with God in the communion of fellowship with the Spirit. As we invite God to move in our souls, however messy, we find that he simultaneously fills us and makes space. We find the support we desire. He always knows exactly what we need even before we do. As he consoles us, we find that our hearts can rest in him.

Loving God, you are the support I desperately need. I have looked for consolation elsewhere, but nothing satisfies like you do. Meet me with your presence that floods my mind with peace and my heart with hope. I rely on you, God.

Tender Relief

Let your steadfast love become my comfort
according to your promise to your servant.

PSALM 119:76 NRSV

God's love is like a tender kiss of mercy. He does not force himself upon us, but he readily comforts us when we make room for him. When we are beaten down by life's storms, battered and bruised, where do we find the respite we so desperately need?

God's loyal love is sweeter than honey; it is more comforting than the arms of our mothers. It is faithful to bind up broken hearts and produce new life out of the rubble. No matter the physical or emotional state we find ourselves in, we can be sure that God is always near. He will wrap us up in his reassuring presence. May the peace of God fill us in every trial we face. He alone offers the deep relief we are looking for.

Merciful God, you are full of lovingkindness to all who come to you. I ask for the comfort of your presence to be my portion today. I need you, Lord. Bring sweet relief as your mercy touches my life. You are always good, and I depend on you.

Courageous Heart

Be of good courage,
And He shall strengthen your heart,
All you who hope in the LORD.

PSALM 31:24 NKJV

There is no easy path in life, no problem-free highway where we can bypass the suffering of this world. We cannot get through this existence avoiding the pain that inevitably touches our lives. God is a refuge for the wanderer, strength to the weak, and healer of the broken.

When Jesus ministered in the last years of his life, he was surrounded by the broken and needy. The sick came to him in droves looking for healing. He welcomed them all, and still he welcomes us in our weakness. Our hopes are set on the Lord, who is our source of strength for everything we face. How could we not be filled with courage when the God of all creation is our supply?

Creator God, I come to you with my little and my lack.
I know that I won't leave your presence in the same way.
God of abundance, fill me with the strength I need for today.
My courage comes from you. You never turn away.
You are my hope.

Trusted Father

Give us a Father's help when we face our enemies.
For to trust in any man is an empty hope.

PSALM 108:12 TPT

Where our trust lies reveals the foundation of our lives. To trust anyone is to put our faith in them. As humans, we all fail and fall short. It is an eventuality—a guarantee—that we will not perfectly fulfill all that we hope or claim. God, though, is perfect in all his ways. He never lies, he never cheats, and he doesn't change his mind. His compassion is longstanding, covering our imperfections with his grace.

Trusting God is a sure bet. He won't let us down, even as we disappoint ourselves. He is so much better than we are. He always offers the help we need without condition. He does not keep an account of our wrongs or a record of what we owe him. He offers support whenever we need it without fail. Let our hearts take hope in him alone.

Father, you are worthy of all my trust. You never fail or waver. You are so good. I look to you today, and I know you do not turn away from me in my seeking. Come and breathe your life in my heart; you are my confident hope.

Constant Prayer

Rejoice in hope,
be patient in tribulation,
be constant in prayer.
ROMANS 12:12 ESV

What a glorious mystery it is that the God of the ages is available to us at all times through prayer. He never disengages from us. He hears every cry—both the spoken and unspoken—of our hearts. We can be encouraged that God never tires of us. Though we grow weary of ourselves and others, he is full of kindness, mercy, and compassion to all who come to him in every single moment.

We cannot catch God at a bad time. He is always listening with love. It is hard for us to comprehend the possibility of something so wonderful when we are faced with limitations everywhere we look. But God is limitless in love. He is abundant in power. He is full of light that chases darkness away. There are no shadows to be found in him. May we never withhold or resist his wonderful love. It is the source of all the delight in our lives.

Wonderful God, you who are rich in mercy and never failing in faithfulness, you are the one I turn to again and again. Today, I won't censor myself with you. I will constantly turn to you in conversation and in prayer. You are the best thing I've ever known. Be near even as I reach out to you.

Adopted

You did not receive a spirit of slavery to fall back into fear, but you have received a spirit of adoption. When we cry, "Abba! Father!" it is that very Spirit bearing witness with our spirit that we are children of God.

ROMANS 8:15-16 NRSV

What a wonderful reality we find within the kingdom of God. We have not been welcomed into an exclusive club when we yield our lives to God. It is not a learning program or a restrictive sect. It is not a working relationship. We have been adopted into a family. We have the rights of sons and daughters of the living God!

Are we living as children of God? Do we truly believe that we are welcomed as dearly loved family, not slaves or servants? The difference is not a subtle one. As children and heirs, we have deep relationship that is based on love and belonging, not on what we have to offer. God is a father, and a good one at that. What we have lacked in our earthly relationships does not rightly reflect the perfection found in the incomparable love of our God.

Abba, I am reminded today that I am your child, not a servant. What a wonderful reminder! Thank you that I can come to you with everything I need. I will not fall into fear today as I approach you, my good Father. I belong to you.

Led by Love

"I will bring the blind by a way they did not know;
I will lead them in paths they have not known.
I will make darkness light before them,
and crooked places straight.
These things will I do for them and not forsake them."

ISAIAH 42:16 NKJV

When plans change and the fear of the unknown settles in, we are left with a choice. We can either give into worry or choose to trust God. We cannot see the way sometimes, and that is okay. We don't need to know how everything will work out; we just need to trust the one who guides us in perfect wisdom. When our lives are shrouded in the mystery of what the future will bring, may we have the courage to rely on God who promises to lead us.

Do you believe that God will work everything out for your good? He leads in love, not by obligation. His affection for you runs deeper than you can imagine. Let yourself lean into his care for you today; he sees everything that you cannot.

Loving God, I am grateful to be led by you. I take comfort in the knowledge that nothing is a mystery to you, nor is any circumstance too much for you to handle. Encourage my heart to hope in your resurrection power over my life.

Children of God

When the right time came, God sent his Son, born of a woman, subject to the law. God sent him to buy freedom for us who were slaves to the law, so that he could adopt us as his very own children.

GALATIANS 4:4-5 NLT

As children of God, we are not slaves to rules but free to rule and reign with Jesus as coheirs of his kingdom. We are taught by a good father, and as we spend more time with him, we resemble him more and more. As we follow in his footsteps, we find that love's expression is diverse and beautiful.

Dearly loved children easily show the confidence they have in their parents' affections. They are able to fully embrace their identities, having been fully loved, accepted, and nurtured. We grow into what we see modeled to us. As children of the living God, we are loved to life so we may love others in the same way—without condition.

Father, you are so wonderful in the way you lead. I look to you as the model I want to live my life by. Fill me with the wonder of a child as I lean into your love today.

Overwhelming Gladness

Do it again!
Those Yahweh has set free will return to Zion
and come celebrating with songs of joy!
They will be crowned with never-ending joy!
Gladness and joy will overwhelm them;
despair and depression will disappear!

ISAIAH 51:11 TPT

Freedom brings with it overwhelming joy! When was the last time you felt the liberation of gladness flood your heart? If you find yourself struggling to even hope for this today, join with Isaiah in declaring, "Do it again!" God is a lifter of heavy burdens and a master restorer. If you are not living in this kind of freedom today, let your heart be encouraged that it is coming. This is not the end of your story.

When we align ourselves with the kingdom of heaven, we will find that even in our darkest days, peace is still our portion. God's presence is the gift of heaven here and now. We are not waiting for a far-off day to know the goodness of our God. His presence is with us now, and it empowers us to life. Even so, we cry out for more. In him, there is abundance of life. Joy is coming.

Yahweh, you set the captives free and liberate those who were bound to darkness. I have tasted this freedom, and I long for more. Fill me with your gladness that causes me to celebrate. Do it again, Lord! You are worthy of all the praise I could ever offer; be glorified.

Double Portion

Return to your stronghold, O prisoners of hope;
today I declare that I will restore to you double.
ZECHARIAH 9:12 NRSV

The Lord is called a refuge and a sanctuary. When we return to him, we will find the rest that we need. Our minds, hearts, and bodies need a safe space where we can let our guard down. When we rest in God's presence, we will find that there is always more than enough.

When was the last time you stopped working for what you want and took time to rest and be rejuvenated? Life can get so busy that it feels frantic. This was not the kind of pace you were meant for. Even when you can't leisurely take your time to fill yourself back up, when you partner with God and come to him, your hope can be restored. Will you return to your source of strength today and let him fill you with all he has for you?

Powerful One, you are the fortress where I retreat to find myself safe and secure. In your presence, I find that I am filled with everything I could ever need. Thank you that you don't give out of scarcity but abundance. I hide myself in your love today. You are the strength of my life.

Resolve

*"Make up your mind not to worry beforehand
how you will defend yourselves."*
LUKE 21:14 NIV

Worry is a temptation to try to figure out what is unknown. How often do we give into the anxiety-laden assumptive scenarios that play out in our minds? What if we were to take control of these thought-storms before they became overwhelming?

It is natural to have what-ifs enter our minds. We can observe these thoughts and then actively lead them by practicing self-direction. This kind of self-control is actually a fruit of the Spirit. It is great practice to observe ourselves and invite God's truth, which brings peace, to our attention. When we meditate on God's Word, we will find that we can differentiate between truth that leads to life and lies that lead to confusion.

Lord, I'm so grateful for the ability to choose. Thank you that your Word leads me to life time and again. When I am lost in confusion and assumptions, would you bring my attention back to your ways? You always have an answer, and with your help, I will be ready for whatever comes.

Answer Me

I hope in You, O Lord;
You will answer, O Lord my God.
PSALM 38:15 NASB

In the Psalms, we see a wide range of the emotions we experience. God can handle all of our complicated feelings even the ups and downs of disappointment and joy. There is nothing we experience that is off-limits to God. We can freely express ourselves without the fear of judgment. His character never wavers; sometimes we reduce God to our own experience. We have a limited scope, but he sees it all. We can find courage in his confidence.

Do you ever feel like you are too much? If so, read through a few psalms today and allow yourself to bring all that you are before God. He will answer you just as he has answered every cry of those who call out to him.

Lord, I come to you with everything I've been carrying. I will not hide my feelings from you today: here I am, with all my baggage. I trust that you will answer me every time I call on you. Don't let my heart sink into despair—I need you!

God My Help

Blessed is he whose help is the God of Jacob,
whose hope is in the Lord his God.

PSALM 146:5 ESV

God is the helper of the broken. When we look at Jacob from the Bible, he did not live an exemplary young life—he was deceitful and greedy. But that was not the end of his story. He made peace with God, and God gave him a new name. God does not turn away the broken and needy; he does not turn a deaf ear to the desperate. When we call on him, he readily answers and clothes us with dignity.

Do you feel like you are beyond the grip of God's goodness? Let him speak his life over you; let your heart find peace with him. What new name has he given you? He will help you no matter how chaotic the situation. He is more compassionate and powerful than you have given him credit for. Let his love change you today.

God of Jacob, my heart takes hope in you. You take broken people and give them new identities. I want to be known as yours just as you are known as my God. I put all my hope in you: come and have your way in my life.

Eagerly Waiting

If we hope for what we do not see,
we eagerly wait for it with perseverance.
ROMANS 8:25 NKJV

Waiting on God takes resolution. Especially when we find that his timing is not ours. We practice perseverance when we hope for what we do not see. When we consider Moses, who led the Israelites into the desert for forty years before they could enter the Promised Land, we can see that their idea of God's timing was not theirs. They thought they would be living in plenty, and yet they were faced with the scarcity of the desert.

Did God leave them? He was with them tangibly and provided the food they needed to be nourished. Just as he was with the Israelites in their waiting, so he is with us in ours. He will not remove his presence from our lives, nor will he cease to provide for every need we have. Let us take hope as we persist in believing God is leading us into his promises in his time.

Faithful God, I confess that waiting has worn down my confidence. When I am discouraged, I will put my hope in you. You are faithfully with me and you will faithfully do what you have promised. You are the fulfillment of my soul's desire and I will press into you.

Stop Striving

Surrender your anxiety!
Be silent and stop your striving
and you will see that I am God.
I am the God above all the nations,
and I will be exalted throughout the whole earth.

PSALM 46:10 TPT

When we are caught in the cycle of stress and worry, it can feel like a cyclone, picking up speed with every anxious thought. It is human nature to try to fix ourselves and our situations, but we cannot cultivate peace in the middle of chaos by tending to every scattered detail. The Lord says, "Be still." The God over all nations is the God who comforts us in our troubles.

Today, will you surrender your anxiety to him? If it takes continually offering the worries to him as they pop up, so be it. This is not a one-time fix but a lifestyle of submission. When the swirl of anxiety begins, take a moment, breathe deeply, and yield to the Lord your maker. Let his peace wash over you.

God of the nations, I yield my heart to you again today. Moment by moment, I lean into your grace that helps me to slow down when my fears begin to ramp up. You are kind and patient and you will never change. I breathe in your peace, letting it fill me up. Thank you for your provision in every moment.

Beautiful

You are altogether beautiful, my darling,
beautiful in every way.
Song of Songs 4:7 nlt

There is nothing quite like being the object of someone's affection. When we allow ourselves to be loved and adored without self-condemnation, our confidence is given the opportunity to grow. When we feel uncomfortable with this sort of love and attention, it reveals what we think about our own worth. Psalm 119 describes how God formed us in our mother's womb; he creatively knit each of us together with purpose and intention.

How convinced are you of God's enjoyment of you? He does not create some people to be loved and others to endure unending rejection. Not only were you created with beauty and purpose, you were made to be loved. God adores you. Will you allow yourself to be encouraged by his devoted affection?

God, I admit that sometimes it is hard for me to believe that I am loveable as I am. Would you speak your words of life over me today and cause me to see myself from your perspective? I yield my self-protection and shame to you today. I don't want to be clouded by these things any longer. Show me who I am to you.

Always the Same

*Jesus Christ is the same yesterday
and today and forever.*

HEBREWS 13:3 NASB

When we consider the incredible life of Jesus, we can clearly see the mercy, kindness, and love of God. His Word says that he remains the same yesterday, today, and forever. His character is constant. We don't have to wonder if Jesus will eventually become fed up with our weakness. Jesus spent the majority of his time with those who were broken and neglected by the world. In fact, the ones he reprimanded were those who thought they had all the answers and were using them to judge others.

Where you have felt less than, be comforted that Jesus draws close to the humble. Let him into those places; you cannot exhaust his compassion. Not today, and not ever.

Jesus, I see now that you do not judge those who are weak and struggling. Meet me in my weakness and strengthen me with your gracious compassion. I won't hold back myself from you today. I will reject the lie that my mess is too much for you. I believe that you heal the wounded. Heal me today, Lord.

April

He has delivered us from the power
of darkness and conveyed us into the
kingdom of the Son of His love.

COLOSSIANS 1:13 NKJV

Faith in Action

*"Even more blessed are all who hear the word of God
and put it into practice."*
LUKE 11:28 NLT

In relationships, our words only count for so much if they are not backed up with action. It is the same in our relationship with God. Where we find ourselves in agreement with the Word of God in what we say, think, or believe, may we be people who live these things out in practical ways. Let us be people who practice what we proclaim.

Consider the last time you gave someone a piece of advice. Was it something you believe to be true? Is it also something that you have been living? Sometimes truth becomes such a part of our psyches that we can easily spout off answers. However, it doesn't always show up as easily in the choices we make in our lives and relationships. Let's be people who put our faith into action.

God, you are so incredibly gracious toward me. I ask for eyes to see where my life is not aligned with your truth. By your Spirit, help me to be empowered to live the truth of your radical love in every area. You are worthy of my trust.

Conviction

Faith is the assurance of things hoped for,
the conviction of things not seen.
HEBREWS 11:1 ESV

Hebrews 11 is known as the faith chapter in the Bible. It recalls those who lived their lives tenaciously clinging to the promises of God, especially when those promises were far off and it was not clear how God would fulfill them. We have the hindsight of history that oversimplifies the process from promise to fulfillment. However, when we consider the humanity of the founders of our faith, we can see the same threads that ran through their lives run through ours.

They faced uncertainty and trials of many kinds although different than those we face. May we echo the faith they clung to, believing that the same God who came through for them will also come through for us. He is faithful to his Word and to his people. May our conviction in God's goodness run deeper than the doubts that shifting circumstances bring.

Holy One, you have been faithful through the ages. You have not changed your character; I take courage in the testimonies of those who have walked with you before me. There is nothing that separates me from your love, and certainly there is no circumstance that can derail your promises. Even as I cling to you, may my faith grow more secure.

Trust Him

You will keep in perfect peace
those whose minds are steadfast,
because they trust in you.
ISAIAH 26:3 NIV

God's loyal love has been proven over and over in the mercy he continuously extends to humanity. Jesus embodied this better than any other example we have been given. His grace toward women, his friendship with the poor and broken, and his disdain for injustice, broke many cultural ideas of who God was. In the same way, God is unfaltering toward us with compassion. May our minds be firmly convinced that God will not change his view of us as his children.

It is natural for a child to trust their dependable, loving parent. We can have the same resolute trust in our good Father. There is an indescribable peace that comes with this kind of deep, reverent faith. May this peace be our portion today and every day.

Yahweh, you continually pour out your love on your children. You are my joy and my portion; fill me with your peace as I hold onto you. You are the one I cling to as if my very life depends on you because it does! You will not disappoint me. You will come through.

Wonderfully Made

*I praise you because you made me
in an amazing and wonderful way.
What you have done is wonderful.
I know this very well.*

Psalm 139:14 NCV

God is Creator. When we look at the world around us, we see the diversity of beauty displayed before our eyes. He could have created one type of tree or one species of flower. We could all be living in the same climate with the same ecosystem. However, this is not the kind of world that God fashioned. In the same beautifully varied way that he created everything in nature, so God also created us uniquely.

Who you are is not accidental. God created you with purpose and with the personality and skills exclusive to you. You are beautifully and wonderfully made! Where you have unfavorably compared yourself to others, may today be the day that you see yourself in all of your wonder. If that seems like a foreign concept, ask God to reveal the greatness that he put within you. Your Maker delights in you.

Creator, give me eyes to see myself the way you do. Remind me that I am fearfully and wonderfully made in your image. I ask that your words of life would pour over me today and that my heart would be open to receive your undiluted love. Tear down every wall that keeps me from this revelation.

Nourished by the Word

If you instruct the brethren in these things,
you will be a good minister of Jesus Christ,
nourished in the words of faith and of the good doctrine
which you have carefully followed.

1 TIMOTHY 4:6 NKJV

It has often been said that you become what you behold. This applies to what you spend your time consuming, how you fill your mind, and what you surround yourself with. How is your soul being fed? It is good and wise to consider both the engaging, intentional sources and also that which becomes noise pollution.

Constant negative programming in the news, though real, does nothing to produce life and hope within our souls. It is the same in social media, the friends we spend time with, and so on. Let's be people who are nourished by the goodness of our God in his Word. Let's choose to listen to things that uplift and challenge our hearts for the better. Let's surround ourselves with people who support us in love. When we are fed in these ways, we will experience the life and health we long for.

Gracious God, I acknowledge that I have not been diligent about what my soul has been consuming. Wash my mind and my heart in your love, cleaning out the cobwebs of confusion. As I feast on your Word, fill my life with the fruit of your Spirit.

Compassionate Father

Praise be to the God and Father of our Lord Jesus Christ,
the Father of compassion and the God of all comfort.
2 CORINTHIANS 1:3 NIV

How do you view God? Is it as some far-off grandfather figure who has arbitrary requirements of you? God is not some being way off in space demanding perfection. Rather, the Word of God reveals him as a father, and not some absent father removed from the lives of his children. He is the Father of compassion and the God of all comfort.

When we consider this, how could we not be drawn to him? He has more than enough understanding of our circumstances. His kindness and consideration are beyond any that we could find in even our closest friend. He is the God of all comfort. Not just some comfort. He has more than enough reassurance to give, and he never tires of consoling us.

Comforter, I easily forget the kindness and compassion you have for me. Somehow, in the craze of life, I find myself drifting from the conviction of your great love. Today, I align myself with your character as a good father. I remember who you have always been—the God of all comfort. Surround me in the loving embrace of your presence.

Strengthened by Love

May our Lord Jesus Christ himself and God our Father,
who loved us and by his grace gave us eternal comfort
and a wonderful hope, comfort you and strengthen you.
2 THESSALONIANS 2:16-17 NLT

When we find ourselves in the abyss of painful circumstances, it can feel as though joy is lost forever. There are some times in life where our experiences will defy the hope that we once held firm. When these dark seasons drag on, how do we cope? How do we survive without drowning in discouragement and despair?

Our God is called our comfort for a reason. He does not expect us to be strong on our own merit. He draws close to the humble, he is a friend to those the world looks down upon, and he offers us strength we could never conjure up. In our weakness, in our pain, we come to him as wounded children who run to their loving caregiver. He is always there to offer the comfort we need.

Loving God, I come to you with my wounds and my pain.
Comfort me with your loving presence and wrap me in your
grace that strengthens me from the inside out. There is no one
who compares to you: what a wonderful Father I have in you!

Never Worry

You will never worry about an attack of demonic forces at night
nor have to fear a spirit of darkness coming against you.

PSALM 91:5 TPT

When fear overtakes us, it can be debilitating. It is no accident that the phrase "do not fear" is used over eighty times in the Bible. God is our confidence and our strength; he is a defender of the weak and a stronghold of security for the vulnerable. When we feel surrounded by darkness and impending doom, we must turn our hearts toward the Lord and trust him.

He gives peace to the restless heart and comfort to the grieved. He sees every detail and nothing you could ever face is too difficult for him to turn around. He will never leave you; he is with you in every moment. You can trust him to take care of you.

Ever-present One, when I am tempted to give in to the overwhelming worries that lurk in the corners of my mind, I will turn to you in surrender. I have seen your faithfulness in my life, and I will trust you to continue to come through time and again. Thank you for your presence that is always with me.

How Long

How long must I worry and feel sad in my heart all day?
How long will my enemy win over me?

PSALM 13:2 NCV

There are some seasons of life where we just can't see the light at the end of the tunnel. Grief, anxiety, and suffering are so familiar that they have become our companions. And yet, when our hearts feel like they can't take any more, God's presence is still our portion.

It is not weakness to feel sadness, and it is not failure to need comfort and encouragement. Let the God of all comfort meet you in the middle of your reality, even in the midst of your waiting. You don't need to be anything other than who you are at this moment, and all he requires is your heart. In the midst of your longing, he is there.

Lord, here I am with my heart laid open before you. I believe that you see me and love me just as I am in this very moment. I am thankful for your love that never leaves me. Strengthen my heart to hold onto you today. Breathe hope into me again.

Perfect Faithfulness

Lord, you are my God;
I will exalt you and praise your name,
for in perfect faithfulness you have done wonderful things,
things planned long ago.
ISAIAH 25:1 NIV

When we consider God's faithfulness, his track record is unmatched. He is trustworthy, and he always follows through with what he says. He is not fickle, and he never acts out of anything but love. His ways are so much higher than ours; he is so much better than we are. His motives are pure and his heart is true.

Today, take a moment to remember how God has shown his kindness and reliability in your life. If you are having trouble pinpointing moments where God came through for you, recount his track record through the words of other testimonies. The Word is full of examples of God's faithfulness, but sometimes it can feel so far removed from our lives. Start looking for evidence of his kindness around you and you will find it.

Lord, you are my God. I know that you will continue to be faithful as you have always been. My heart takes hope in your great goodness today. You have done wonderful things, and I believe that I will continue to see your kindness displayed in my life.

Waiting on the Lord

Now, O Lord, what do I wait for?
My hope is in you.
PSALM 39:7 NRSV

In the busyness of everyday life, it takes practice to slow down. Waiting patiently has become a foreign concept to many of us. With the Lord, though, so much richness is found in the stillness. When we take a few (or more) moments to disconnect from the frenetic pace of our lives, we find peace in the quiet.

Waiting is not always motionless, nor is it inactive. A posture of hope keeps us trusting in the Lord and his Word even as our timelines adjust. When we are in places in between and need to lean into love's pace, we have the opportunity to calibrate our hearts with God's perfect peace. It is always available and always in a measure of abundance.

Good Father, I trust that as I wait on you, you will fill me up with the perfect peace of your presence. You are full of compassion at every moment, and I lean into your care as I put all my hope in you. I trust you to do what you said you would do in your perfect timing.

Momentary Troubles

This light momentary affliction is preparing for us an eternal weight of glory beyond all comparison, as we look not to the things that are seen but to the things that are unseen. For the things that are seen are transient, but the things that are unseen are eternal.

2 CORINTHIANS 4:17-18 ESV

The troubles we face are only momentary in comparison with the eternal hope we hold onto. When this world has passed away and we are on the other side of eternity, the fulfillment of joy will be ours. There will be no more worry, no more tears of sadness. The glory of our God will be the light that never dims, and we will find ourselves fully alive.

Circumstances change. Think through your life over the last several years; how many of those years were identical? Does what you worried about five years ago still hold the same concern? God is the same yesterday, today, and forever. What you are walking through today will not take you out. You will get through this.

Holy One, I set my eyes on you, the one who never changes. I have been so caught up in the shifting circumstances of my life, letting stress overwhelm me. Calm the anxiety in my heart. Today I fix my mind on you, my eternal hope and my joy.

Delivered from Darkness

*He has rescued us from the kingdom of darkness
and transferred us into the Kingdom of his dear Son.*
COLOSSIANS 1:13 NLT

God is light and all things are made alive in him. When we align our lives with his, we find freedom to live out his incredible love. We have been delivered from the darkness that once covered and imprisoned us. We live in his light even in the midst of our troubles and suffering. Our hearts can dwell in perfect peace during the storms of life.

Where you have felt unseen and unheard, take heart that there is nothing hidden from the gaze of your loving Father. He can and will meet you in the middle of your chaos and bring the peace you desperately long for. Find your home in the kingdom of love where there is a place for you. Darkness cannot keep you away.

Deliverer, I have known your goodness in my life before, and I believe that I will continue to see your faithful love poured out. Thank you that I have a place in your kingdom of love and that it can never be stolen! In your light I come alive.

Heart's Delight

Your laws are my treasure;
they are my heart's delight.
PSALM 119:11 NLT

When we find ourselves at a loss for what to do or where to turn, there is so much wisdom to be found in God. In his Word, we find instructions for life that breathe hope into our weary hearts. Living submitted to God's ways, we are filled with everything we need.

God's ways are perfect, and he makes no mistakes. When we are overwhelmed by the thought of tomorrow, it is easy to forget that God's faithfulness displayed throughout the ages is the same faithfulness with us today. He will continue to be faithful in all of our tomorrows. Let us find our peace in him. May our hearts find true delight in God in every season.

God over all, you always offer grace when I need it. I am so aware of my need for you. Fill me with your presence that awakens my heart to hope in you. You have been faithful and you will always be. Lead me in your perfect wisdom and be my heart's delight.

Shining Light

*"Let your light shine before others,
that they may see your good deeds
and glorify your Father in heaven."*

MATTHEW 5:16 NIV

In the light of God's presence, we shine. Just as the moon has no light of its own and yet it shines brightly at night, so do we reflect the light of God. We do not depend on our own goodness, but God's, to stand out in our lives. As we walk on the path of God's love, we are changed into his likeness.

What a relief it is that we don't rely on our own strength. We are empowered to live as Christ as we lean into his grace that is like an ever-flowing fountain, replenishing our thirsty souls. Today we have an opportunity to press into love; how could we not reflect God's heart if we live out of that place?

Father of light, you are the source of all life. I lean into your heart of love, knowing that as I receive out of the overflow of your heart, I have more than enough to give away to others. Thank you that your abundance is the measure I live out of, not my own scarcity. Be glorified in my life.

Lifelong Love

Surely your goodness and love will be with me all my life,
*and I will live in the house of the L*ORD *forever.*

PSALM 23:6 NCV

God has never withheld his love from us. He is full of compassion for us, meeting us at every turn with the kindness of a good father. This love that covers us in our triumphs and successes is the same love that carries us through our darkest days.

There is no moment, no season, and no circumstance where God removes his presence from us. In him we find everything we need for life, and not just survival. All the days of our lives we are wrapped in the kindness of our God. Where we have trouble seeing his perfect character toward us, may we have eyes to see where he is already working things out for our good.

Loving Father, I am covered by your grace that empowers me to live with my hope set on you. Your presence is my portion today and forever. Fill me with your perfect love. If I am overwhelmed by anything today, may it be with your kindness!

God's People

The Lord will not abandon His people on account of His great name,
because the Lord has been pleased to make you a people for Himself.

1 SAMUEL 12:22 NASB

Looking in the Word, we see evidence of God's loyal love to his people. He does not give up or turn away from those who seek him. And even if we turn away, he warmly and willingly welcomes us back! Consider the parable of the prodigal son. He left his father's house, going his own way, squandering his inheritance. When he returned, he came as a broken man left with no other options, covered in shame.

What was the father's response? Was it a cold shoulder or an, "I told you so"? No, he ran out to meet his broken son, covered him in his own robe, and called for a lavish celebration. The son was ready to beg to live on his father's land as a servant, yet he was completely restored as an honored son. In the same way, we come to God with all of our shame and he covers us in his love, restoring us as his children and heirs.

Gracious Father, you are full of mercy and kindness to all who come to you. I will not stay away. I approach you with the humility of my circumstances and the confidence of your child. Even as I question how you could ever accept me as I am, I freely come to you again. Wrap me in your unfailing love.

Filled by Power

May the God of hope fill you with all joy and peace in believing,
so that you may abound in hope by the power of the Holy Spirit.
ROMANS 15:13 NRSV

When doubts cause confusion to fill our minds, and hope feels like a lost luxury of the innocent, it is hard to find strength to persevere in belief. What then? Do we will change into existence? Do we punish ourselves because we have missed the mark yet again? Do we disqualify ourselves as not good enough?

Our God is not a taskmaster. He does not require perfection— not ever! He does not expect us to transform into carbon copies of Jesus. We were created as unique reflections of his love. It is the power of the Holy Spirit, our constant companion, that fills us with everything we need to live a life of faith, joy, peace, and hope. Where there is lack in our lives, there is space for an invitation of God's power to permeate us, to change us.

Holy Spirit, I invite you into my lack today. There is so much. Yet you are the hope that fills me and empowers me to persevere in believing for breakthrough. Bring peace to my mind and heart today. I welcome you to come and change me again from the inside out.

Pause

As I thought of you I moaned,
"God, where are you?"
I'm overwhelmed with despair
as I wait for your help to arrive.
Pause in his presence.
PSALM 77:3 TPT

There are times in life where there is no silver lining. We cannot create goodness out of what looks like desolation and destruction. It is not a failure to be desperate. When we can't see how anything can grow out of the devastation of our lives, we do not need to pretend to be hopeful.

Let us come to God, asking him the questions that lurk in the corners of our mind. "Where are you" may be the cry that comes out. When all seems lost, let us take the time to wait on him. This is an invitation to remember who God is. Not who he was or will be, but who he is right now. Yes, it's all the same because he is unchanging, but sometimes our hearts need the reminder that he is with us, right here and right now. Let's take a cue from the psalmist and pause in God's presence.

Everlasting God, you are the same yesterday, today, and forever. As I come to you with the desperation of a heart that is overwhelmed, I take the time to pause before you. Come, Holy Spirit, and fill me with the power of your presence as I cry out for more of you.

Don't Fret

Be still in the presence of the LORD,
and wait patiently for him to act.
Don't worry about evil people
who prosper or fret about their wicked schemes.

PSALM 37:7 NLT

In this life, we cannot control what other people choose. We can only command our own thoughts, hearts, and lives. With that in mind, how we choose to direct ourselves in the middle of chaos can determine the peace, or lack of it, within us.

When was the last time you stilled your thoughts and offered the Lord your attention in the middle of the stresses and worry storms of life? He is faithfully with you. As you cultivate a heart of surrender, choosing to direct your mind and heart toward him, he will fill you with the peace you long for. His presence is always accessible. Where you have felt haste to act in your own defense, step back and let your protector fight for you.

Defender, you are the one who keeps me in perfect peace while the storms of life rage around me. I still my heart before you today, offering you the space to speak your words of life over me again. I submit my mind to you. Fill me with the lifegiving stillness of your presence.

Freedom Now

The Lord is the Spirit,
and where the Spirit of the Lord is,
there is freedom.
2 CORINTHIANS 3:17 NIV

Where there is freedom, there is a feeling of open space—of opportunity. There is freedom to choose, freedom to live. When God created Adam and Eve in the garden, he gave them freedom from the beginning. He also gave instruction and wisdom. Friendship with God was the design, and it was their reality.

Friendship is still God's design, and it is our reality in the freedom that Christ paid for with his very life. We don't need to wait for an unknown time and place to experience the original liberty of walking with God without anything standing in our way. We have the Spirit of God with us, and there is nothing that can separate us from his vast love.

Holy Spirit, you are the companion that encourages my soul and strengthens my heart to keep going in this life. I am so grateful for the freedom that you bring; it is always available and always more than enough. Bring fresh revelation of the liberty I have in you today!

New Life

There is hope for a tree, if it is cut down,
that it will sprout again,
and that its tender shoots will not cease.

JOB 14:7 NKJV

There is no situation so grim that God can't turn it around. When we consider the life of Job, all the tragedies that he faced and the loss he dealt with, we may be tempted to write off his experience as exceptional. As long as we are in this world, we will go through struggles and suffering. There's no doubt about it. The levels of pain may differ in our lives, but we all experience it.

Our hopes are not anchored to our happiness or to shifting circumstances. Our hope is secured in Christ and his resurrection. He overcame death—what then is left? Our deepest fears are covered by the great love of our God. We are safe and secure in him. He resurrects what was dead and brings new life to all he touches. We are his, and he will surely revive us in his mercy, causing life to grow where we only see barrenness.

God of all life, breathe hope into my heart again today. In you, even what was dead comes to life. You are the master reviver and rebuilder. I trust you to do the impossible in my life. Only you can.

Seen

Behold, the eye of the LORD is on those who fear him,
on those who hope in his steadfast love.

PSALM 33:18 ESV

The God of the entire universe is the same God who knows every detail of your life. There is no aspect too insignificant that he overlooks it. What matters to you, matters to him. He draws near even now with his presence, covering you with his great love. You need not worry or run away—his compassion for you is greater than your fear.

What a wonderful King! His love is more reliable than the rising and setting of the sun. We take for granted that the stars will shine at night and that the tides will shift during the day. Yet, God's unfailing mercy is more constant than the most reliable workings of nature. Let us take hope in the loyal love of our Father.

Lord, I am reminded that my life does not go unnoticed by you. Comfort me as I look to you today. Bring resolution where I only see confusion and open-ended questions. Fill me with the confidence of your affection through the power of your presence. I need you.

I Will Praise

I will hope continually,
and will praise you yet more and more.
PSALM 71:14 NRSV

Our hope is not in the mountains or the valleys we tread. It is not found in the circumstances of our lives. Our anticipation lies in the working out of God's faithful character. He who is slow to anger, abounding in love to all, who makes all things new in his mercy—he is our great confidence. When our hearts begin to waver, may they be strengthened by his nearness.

When we look at our lives and see evidence of God's goodness, how can we keep ourselves from praising him? Will we withhold our gratitude, overlooking instances of his mercy woven through our stories? Or will we posture our hearts to honor him? May we offer him what we have, and may he fill us with the wonder of children as he continually meets us with his mercy and loves us to life.

Faithful One, encourage my heart today in your loyal love. You never stop working. Give me eyes to see where you've planted your goodness in my life. My heart is open to you, Lord; come and have your way!

My Confidence

You are my hope; O Lord God,
You are my confidence from my youth.

PSALM 71:5 NASB

As children, we learn to value what is modeled. If in our families we are taught the importance of self-reliance, then we will live as those who have to get things done on our own. If we are taught the significance of honesty, we will most likely tell the truth throughout our lives. When we learn to rely on God, we will find that our hearts trust him as he faithfully leads us.

It is never too late to learn how to live submitted to God's mercy and compassion. He is a restorer of all things even time! May we find that as we rely on God we are changed into his likeness. May our hearts find strength in his unfailing love, and may his peace be our daily portion. He is more than able to make our lives fruitful no matter the length of them. He is our true hope.

Lord God, you are amazing in your leadership. You bring healing and restoration to everything you touch. Come touch my life with your lifegiving presence again. You are my hope, and my greatest confidence is in you.

Restoration

"The blind see again, the crippled walk, lepers are cured,
the deaf hear, the dead are raised back to life,
and the poor and broken now hear of the hope of salvation!"

MATTHEW 11:5 TPT

What a wonderful God we have! He heals the sick, brings the dead to life, and saves the destitute. These are not just nice ideas. His power touches our lives in tangible ways. If we struggle to see his goodness, let us invite him to do what only he can do. He is lifter of the broken; surely he will meet us.

There is no time limit to his mercy. His promises do not have an expiration date. Today is the day of salvation. Today is the day we are given; it is all we have. May we cry out from our hearts straight to the heart of our good Father who always hears us. If we have places of brokenness in our lives, we can be sure that these areas are waiting to be touched by God.

Healer, I ask for you to restore me today. Touch my mind, my shattered spirit, and my body with your healing love. I cannot escape your grasp. Come near and revive me!

Delivered Again

He delivered us from such a deadly peril, and he will deliver us.
On him we have set our hope that he will deliver us again.

2 CORINTHIANS 1:10 ESV

God's character never changes. He who healed will heal again. He who forgave will forgive again. The one who delivered his people will once again deliver them. He is better than we give him credit for. We cannot exhaust his all-encompassing mercy and compassion. May our hearts take courage in the account that history tells of his goodness. That same goodness is ours.

When our hopes are set in the faithfulness of God, they will not be disappointed. Where we have struggled to hold onto optimism about our futures and present circumstances, let us yield our hearts in surrender once again. When we stir up our histories with God, we see with eyes of confidence, knowing that where God came through, he will come through again. He doesn't tire of helping us.

Good God, you are my constant help. When I remember your goodness displayed in my life, I can't help but be encouraged. May my heart find its confidence in your character not in the overwhelming worries of my present circumstances. You are so good!

Eager Expectation

It is my eager expectation and hope that I will not be put to shame in any way, but that by my speaking with all boldness, Christ will be exalted now as always in my body, whether by life or by death.

PHILIPPIANS 1:20 NRSV

Where do our expectations find their fulfillment? Is it in our own strength and reliability? Even with excellence as our pattern, we falter. God is our covering, and he is perfect in all his ways. He will not let us be put to shame even as we walk through pain and troubles.

May our hearts find their strength in the promises of God who is faithful. With our eyes set on him, we will not be disappointed, for he is our greatest reward. We can never reach the end of his lovingkindness, and we will never deplete his compassion. We will know and see him in all his glory when this short life is over. Every hope pales in comparison to his grandeur!

Holy One, you are the expectation of my heart. Though I walk through the valley, I know that you are with me. I only see part of the picture, and you consider the whole. I trust you to guide me in your unfailing love all the days of my life. Be my strength and the joy of my life!

Cared For

*Give all your worries to him,
because he cares about you.*

1 PETER 5:7 NCV

When Jesus referred to God, he spoke of him as a father. The relationship they had was one of closeness and trust. Through the death and resurrection of Christ, we were welcomed into the same connection. The good, kind, faithful Father of Jesus is also our merciful, compassionate Father.

We don't need to carry our worries around like obligatory badges of adulthood. We are children of the Living God, with access to his help at every moment. He never meant for us to strive for survival on our own. When we are connected to the Father, relying on him for the help we need, we find that worry is just wasted energy. Our good Father can handle everything—we need only trust him and follow his wisdom.

Father, you are the one I rely on in every situation. Here are all of my worries and fears. You can have them all. I don't want to sway from dread to hope like a pendulum. Be my rock and firm foundation. You are my help, and you are faithful. I lean into your support today.

Peaceful and Secure

*"My people will live free from worry
in secure, quiet homes of peace."*
ISAIAH 32:18 TPT

God is full of peace. He does not stir up dissension or cause conflicts. He is the great unifier. Though we live in a world full of chaos and reckless decisions, God is the opposite. He brings order and leads in perfect love and wisdom. As we bind ourselves to his goodness, we find the rest we long for in his presence.

There is no situation so messed up that God cannot bring redemption from it. He is the best at bringing stability to confusion. We are his people, called by his name. We have been adopted into his family. As his children, we are invited to live in the atmosphere of his good nature. Where he is, we can be confident of our safety. He keeps us and holds us. Let us not lose heart or let fear overtake us.

God of peace, you are steady and sure. Your kindness is unmoving, your heart pure. With you, I know that I am covered. I don't need to worry about a thing. May my heart be filled with your peace today as I walk in your ways.

May

You will keep in perfect peace

those whose minds are steadfast,

because they trust in you.

ISAIAH 26:3 NIV

No More Tears

God's dwelling place is now among the people,
and he will dwell with them.
"He will wipe every tear from their eyes.
There will be no more death"
or mourning or crying or pain,
for the old order of things has passed away.

REVELATION 21:3-4 NIV

As we wait for God's kingdom to invade earth just as it is in heaven, may our hearts find comfort and hope in his presence with us here and now. Every painful circumstance is temporary; suffering will not last forever. Even as we endure the hardships of this life, God's compassion can cover us and carry us into the peace of his heart.

Though weeping may last for a season, we are not destined for perpetual sadness. Even now we have God with us—his presence is tangible through the Holy Spirit. He strengthens us when we are weak, comforts us in our sorrow, and helps us in our need. Though the ultimate freedom from pain is coming, we have tastes of this glorious reality available through the nearness of our God and King. He is full of mercy.

God, strengthen my heart to trust and my body to rest as I take refuge in you. In my sorrow, I know that your comfort is the only thing that can truly ease my agony. I lean on your grace, God. Show up today in power.

Covered

You bless the righteous, O LORD;
you cover them with favor as with a shield.
PSALM 5:12 NRSV

When was the last time you felt the uncomfortable feeling that is associated with vulnerability? When you feel exposed, God is closer than you know. He covers you. He blesses the righteous, and all it takes to be considered righteous is to be submitted to him. He is a refuge for the weak; find your rest in him.

Where you have felt weak, needy, and completely ill fitted, trust that God more than makes up for what you lack. He does not expect you to have it all together. He does not require perfection. His mercy meets you right where you are, and he covers you with his overwhelming love. It covers everything—you don't need to worry about a thing. Look up from your need and see that he is full of abundance.

Lord, you are the hope of my heart. I am extremely aware of my own shortcomings, but all of it pales in comparison to your great love. Cover me today. Meet every need by your abounding grace. Your provision is better than any of my own plans.

Lifted Up

*Humble yourselves in the sight of the Lord,
and He will lift you up.*

JAMES 4:10 NKJV

God is close to the humble, and he lifts up those who fall. When we think that we are too far gone, that is just when we find that God's abundant mercy brings us back from the brink into love once again. He never gives up, and he is not worried by the cares that overwhelm us.

We can never fall outside of God's reach. He does not roll his eyes when he finds we've wandered from his path of love again. He never leaves us, and it is his nature to relentlessly love us to life over and over again. We couldn't exhaust his mercy even if we tried. May we find our home in the arms of our good shepherd.

Loving God, your mercy knows no end. What a marvelous thought! Invade my life with your unfailing love that never lets go of me. Let your loyal heart encompass every failure, every shame, and every downfall in my life. I am nothing without you.

Continue Strong

Be alert.
Continue strong in the faith.
Have courage, and be strong.
Do everything in love.
1 CORINTHIANS 16:13-14 NCV

When we look at the life of Jesus, we find that everything he did in his ministry, he did out of love. He was the pure reflection of the Father. In his humility, he served those who should have served him. He laid down his life in love over and over again. He chose the way of peace, mercy, and kindness when confronted with troubles.

As we follow in his steps, love's example is our primary purpose. We find courage as we press into the presence of our God. The strength to keep going is not found in our own motivation but in being filled by God's great mercy every day. His compassion never fails to satisfy us. Let's not give up coming to him—his abundance never wanes!

Merciful God, you are the source of everything I need. Even as I feel my strength and resolve weakening, I come to you. You are the giver of good gifts. Lead me in your love each new day. Guide me in your mercy.

Love Remains

Faith, hope, and love abide, these three;
but the greatest of these is love.
1 CORINTHIANS 13:13 ESV

Just when we think that the love of God has become rote, he comes in the power of his presence. His presence changes everything. It goes beyond our logical understanding and brings peace where there was chaos. His presence heals our minds and bodies. We cannot be touched by God and be unchanged. We have not drained God's resources, for he is the source of every good thing, and he never runs dry.

These three will always remain: faith, hope, and love. Where these abide, there God is. We can be sure that when our hearts are full of these, God is alive in us. Where we lack them, we need only ask. He freely gives to all who request his presence. In his nearness, we find our hearts come alive in love. Today is a fresh start.

Faithful One, you always show up in power. You don't grow tired or weary, dragging your feet. Your joy is abundant even as I barely glimpse at you. Come and let faith, hope, and love fill my heart. You are so good.

Renewed Strength

*"You were tired out by the length of your road,
Yet you did not say, 'It is hopeless.'
You found renewed strength,
Therefore you did not faint."*

ISAIAH 57:10 NASB

The road of life at times feels extremely short and unbearably long. In seasons of suffering, it can feel like there is no end to the pain and sorrow. It is important to remember that God's character is absolutely unchanging. Though our circumstances shift, his mercy never does.

We will surely find our strength renewed along the way. As he reminds us of his faithfulness, God continues to direct our path. Even as we stumble, he lifts us up. As long as it is called today, there is hope. The journey of life is not over; defeat has not overcome us. We are led in love every day, with no exceptions!

God, you are my strength. When my resources run dry, I find that I have everything I need and more in your presence. Fill me today. Lead me on in your kindness. I lean on you as if my very life depends on it.

Freedom of Grace

Sin is no longer your master,
for you no longer live under the requirements of the law.
Instead, you live under the freedom of God's grace.

ROMANS 6:14 NLT

In the light of God's love, we have been set free. We have been perfected in Jesus. We don't rely on our own abilities to do well or to perfectly perform. We are not bound by the strict confines of perfection—we would fail at it anyhow. Thank God for his mercy and grace that holds space for us when we fail. In our faltering, we are fully loved and known.

God does not turn away from the weak or the struggling. In fact, he draws near to the humble and refreshes them with his comfort. Living under the freedom of God's grace, we find that it is not so devastating when we mess up. There is mercy extended at every opportunity. We don't need to live in the shame of our mistakes; rather, we live within the liberty of loyal love.

God, you are full of grace that never runs out. As I cling to you, I find love that lifts me out of every situation that weighs me down. You are so much better than anyone I've ever known. Purify me in your presence again today.

Submitted to Christ

My God, I want to do what you want.
Your teachings are in my heart.
PSALM 40:8 NCV

The teachings of God are full of purpose. They reflect his good nature. His perfect character is on display clearly in his law of love. As we look to the instruction of Jesus, we find that God's ways are different than our own. Instead of seeking revenge, Jesus humbly extended forgiveness to all. Instead of success and riches, he rejected them in favor of being close to the needy and the broken. Instead of taking things by force, he peacefully offered his way as an option.

When we learn from Jesus and put his law of love into practice, we will find that the fruit is sweeter than any we have ever known. His love satisfies in a way that no amount of worldly success can. Notoriety is fleeting, but a life of honor and purpose no one can take away. May we submit our hearts to Jesus, knowing that his way is so much better than our own.

My God, you are the one I look to in my confusion. I trust you as I submit my life to you once again. I have to believe that you are making something good out of the situations I am walking through. With your help, I will walk in your way of love, finding fulfillment in your nearness and in the fruit of a life submitted to you.

Immeasurably More

*To him who is able to do immeasurably
more than all we ask or imagine,
according to his power that is at work within us,
to him be glory...for ever and ever! Amen.*

EPHESIANS 3:20-21 NIV

In the midst of trial and change, when requests are ever on our minds, it can feel like we are running out God's patience. We continually ask for the overwhelming needs in our lives to be met. But this isn't the case! God is full of patience, and he delights in us whenever we come to him. When we live in a posture of open relationship with the Lord, both giving and receiving, we find that he is abundantly better than our wildest hopes.

Have you been holding back from bringing your questions and needs to God? If so, let today be the day you lay it all out before him. It doesn't matter how many times you've asked—bring your requests to God. He never tires of your voice; his power is at work within you. As you pour out your heart to him today, take some time to receive his perspective and love for you. His thoughts toward you are full of tender affection.

Holy One, you are the one I come to in every season of the soul. In times of need, I desperately come to you. Today again, I lay out my heart before you—every part! You see the obvious and the hidden spaces, so why would I try to pretend that they aren't there? Meet me, Lord.

Free from Anxiety

"Remain passionate and free from anxiety and the worries of this life. Then you will not be caught off guard by what happens."

LUKE 21:34 TPT

It takes practice to remain worry-free in this hectic world. When plans change and we need to adjust our expectations, it is easy to fall into the trap of despair and the swirl of anxiety. When we rely on our circumstances to find our happiness or our stability, we will be sorely disappointed.

Let today be the day you come to God with all your cares—all your worries and anxieties. He can handle them, and you were never meant to bear them on your own. You will find the passion and freedom you're looking for in God alone. You cannot carry yourself through the storms of life and thrive. Let go and lean into him today.

Savior, I rely on your strength to meet me in my weakness. I am not strong enough to get rid of the anxiety I feel. Instead, I come to you and ask that you would fill me with the power of your presence. Let your perfect love drive out every fear that keeps me stuck. Thank you, Lord!

Sanctuary

The Lord also will be a refuge for the oppressed,
a refuge in times of trouble.
Those who know Your name will put their trust in You;
for You, Lord, have not forsaken those who seek You.

PSALM 9:9-10 NKJV

God is a hiding place for those who need shelter from the storms of life. He is a strong and sure foundation, immovable. He is a wrap-around refuge, impenetrable. How could we but put our trust in him when he has proven himself faithful over and over again?

He does not leave those who come to him to fend for themselves. He does not abandon the heartsick and broken. He tends to the wounded, healing them and caring for them. He mends; he does not tear apart. Does this image of God resonate with what we believe to be true? Let us run to him in our time of need. He is full of hospitality and warmth to all who pursue him.

Protector, you have been my hiding place before, and I will not hesitate to make my home in your love. Where I have felt hesitant to approach you, I remember that you are merciful. I come to you just as I am, broken state and all. Heal me, Lord, as I rest in you.

Longing

My soul longs for your salvation;
I hope in your word.
PSALM 119:81 ESV

In the waiting, there is always longing. Sometimes aching, other times more wishful, the longing of the in-between is as real as the promise itself. The now and not yet is the tension of living with the hope of what is to come while experiencing a different reality. This can be discouraging if it is only the promise of something to come that we find fulfillment in.

Thankfully, in the waiting God is with us—Emmanuel. He never leaves, and he has given us his life-giving presence, not only to sustain us but also to fill us with the abundance of his love. In the expectation of more to come, may we not lose sight of what we have right now.

Emmanuel, you are God with us. You are the hope of every longing heart, and I know that everything I need can be found in you. Even as I wait on your promises, I find joy in you, for in you is the fulfillment of every hope I have. Meet me here and now and remind me of your overwhelming goodness.

Free Indeed

"If the Son sets you free, you are truly free."
JOHN 8:36 NLT

God is not in the business of setting captives free only to enslave them to his purposes. We have been freed by his great love and mercy so that we are uncontrolled and uninhibited by fear. There are no catches in his love. He does not have a hidden agenda. His love is pure and unblemished. He is not manipulative in love. He has always been about companionship.

As lovers of God, we are free to follow him. We are free to choose how we will live our lives. We are free. Do we truly live as those who have been liberated from dread and immorality? In the light of God's love, we are able to see truth where before we were confused by lies. God's mercy is abundantly better than we can imagine.

Son of God, thank you for freedom. Where I have been bound up by fear and worried about taking a wrong step, flood my heart with your perfect love that brings with it the clarity of your wisdom.

Wisdom Found

Know that wisdom is thus for your soul;
If you find it, then there will be a future,
and your hope will not be cut off.
PROVERBS 24:14 NASB

When we search for wisdom in our lives, we can be sure that we will find it. Why would we attempt to find it anywhere other than the source of wisdom itself? God's ways are not outdated, nor are they out of touch. His ways are always the best, and his solutions are full of perfect understanding.

If you find that you're lacking in hope for your future, lean into the presence of God today. He is full of answers for all who ask him. May you be filled to overflowing with his love that pushes back the fears that keep worries swirling around your head. May he be the peace that brings clarity to every confusion. He is reliable. He will come through for you.

God of all wisdom, I need you to lead me into life. I have reached the end of my knowledge; I'm desperate to know what your solutions for my life are. Bring peace as I wait on you. With your love alive in my heart, I will confidently walk forward toward hope.

Encouraged to Hope

Whatever was written in former days was written for our instruction, so that by steadfastness and by the encouragement of the scriptures we might have hope.

ROMANS 15:4 NRSV

Looking through the Word of God, we find common themes that reveal God's character. His faithfulness is unquestionable when we consider how he always accomplishes what he sets out to do. We see that mercy triumphs over judgment every time. When people cried out to God throughout history, he consistently answered them. He still does.

Let us not become weary in discouragement. God who was with the Israelites, with David, with Ruth, with Paul, is the same God who is with us. He has not changed his mind about humanity—we are still the work of his hands and the object of affection within his heart. What encouragement we can find in remembering how God has come through for us in the past. He will come through again!

Faithful One, you are the God who never changes. In faithfulness is still how you operate. May my heart be encouraged as I walk in the way of the truth of your love as many have before me. Fill me with your hope.

Beauty from Within

Your beauty should come from within you—the beauty of a gentle and quiet spirit that will never be destroyed and is very precious to God.

1 PETER 3:4 NCV

God does not judge us based on our outer appearance. He is much more concerned with the state of our hearts than how put together we appear. A beggar with a heart of devotion and love is more beautiful than a shallow princess decked in the world's finest jewels.

Your spirit is precious to God. Don't neglect the impact of your heart's attitude. When you keep your heart open in humility and submission to love, you cannot go wrong. Don't be discouraged when others overlook you; there is no need to compare yourself to others. You are uniquely and wonderfully made, and you have infinite worth to your Maker!

God my Maker, you know my heart better than even I do. Would you fill me with your love that keeps me soft and humble before you and others? I yield myself to you, knowing that beauty is much deeper than the skin. May the beauty of your work within me radiate from the inside out.

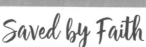

Saved by Faith

Believe on the Lord Jesus Christ,
and you will be saved,
you and your household.

ACTS 16:31 NKJV

When we believe in Jesus, it is more than just choosing in our minds to agree with what we've been told about him. We live aligned with his kingdom truth. We offer him our loyalty and commitment. We trust and rely on his goodness in our lives even as we give ourselves to being united with his character.

When you consider your lifestyle, where do your loyalties lie? When you look at the fruit of your life, is it reflective of what you say you believe? Without judgment, look objectively at what your life reveals as the things you are convinced of. If there is discrepancy between what you say you believe and how you live, take this opportunity to ask why. Invite the Lord into this part of your processing and allow him to show you the truth of his love over you.

Good God, in looking at my life, I see that there are holes and areas where I cannot see your goodness at work. There are pieces of me that are desperate and searching. I know that nothing is outside of your realm even the ugly parts of me that feel like too much. I yield my heart to you again. May my life be marked by loyalty to you and your love.

Without Hindrance

*He proclaimed the kingdom of God
and taught about the Lord Jesus Christ—
with all boldness and without hindrance!*
ACTS 28:31 NIV

When we look at the life of Paul, we find that he did not have it easy. When he was converted on the road to Damascus, he could not deny the life-changing power of Jesus. Previously, he had tortured those who had claimed Christ as God. After this experience, Paul was forever changed. He devoted his life to preaching the truth of God's powerful love through Jesus all the days of his life.

Paul was imprisoned, mocked, and beaten over the course of his ministry. He did not consider that any of this meant that he was living a life outside of God's control—on the contrary! He considered the suffering he endured to be part of the cost of following Jesus. He continually encouraged others not to be surprised by it but to count the cost as an honor. Suffering was not a hindrance to Paul's life and ministry. Can we say the same?

God, you are gracious in your ways. When I don't understand the chaos of my circumstances, may I not let the whys distract me from whose I am. I belong to you, and I count everything as loss compared to knowing you. Fill me with your life-giving grace today.

Common Ground

When I am with those who are weak, I share their weakness,
for I want to bring the weak to Christ.
Yes, I try to find common ground with everyone,
doing everything I can to save some.
1 CORINTHIANS 9:22 NLT

There is a bond that develops in shared experience. Mutual understanding builds trust that allows us to open to one another in sincerity. Jesus did not live as a recluse on this earth or as someone who was out of reach. As the King of Kings, he could have lived in riches, but that is not what he chose. He humbled himself, always welcoming friendship with the lowest in society.

Jesus was not exclusive in who he let approach him, so may we feel free to come to him with all of our messes. He has already seen it all. We have not been disqualified from knowing and following him because of our weakness. He welcomes us in. In the same way, we show his love in our lives when we share in the experiences of those around us.

Humble King, you are incredible in the compassion you exhibit to all who turn to you. There is no sin too great, no darkness too overbearing, no sickness too beyond your reach. In your kindness, may I find the grace to live your embodied compassion toward myself and others. You are so generous!

Saving Grace

My soul, why would you be depressed?
Why would you sink into despair?
Just keep hoping and waiting on God, your Savior.
For no matter what, I will still sing with praise,
for living before his face is my saving grace!

PSALM 42:5 TPT

When we're feeling low, it is hard to be motivated. We may find ourselves sinking into despair as we consider our circumstances. It is not failure to have a bad day or to feel overwhelmed; we don't need to feel shame about this.

At the same time, we have been given the gift of leadership over our minds and hearts. When the troubles we face outweigh the hope we have, let us direct our soul's eyes back to the one who set the world in motion. He is still faithful. He is still working. He is still worthy. Today is an opportunity to praise him in the "not yet."

Savior, oh how I need you! You see the internal struggle I am faced with: as I choose to trust, hope, and wait on you, even when my soul is sinking, would you fill me with the encouragement I so desperately need? Thank you for your faithful presence. I know you will come through again. I praise you today.

Future Hope

*Surely there is a future,
and your hope will not be cut off.*
PROVERBS 23:18 ESV

The hope of the righteous is like a firmly rooted tree. No storm of life will tear it down because God is the keeper. In areas of your life where you struggle to see any possibility that is not filled with destruction or despair, may God give you his perspective.

God is the restorer of all broken things; he specializes in bringing beauty out of the ashes of destruction. Where you see an end, God sees a new beginning. He is constantly making all things new—even today, even in your life. You have not reached the end of his goodness; you have not tapped the limits of his mercy and grace. Surely there is a bright future for you as you walk through the pain of the present.

Good God, you are the one who turns my mourning into dancing. I know that I will see your goodness in my life again—I have to hold onto that hope. Fill me with your grace that empowers me. I yield my mind and heart to yours today. Fill me with the light of your presence.

Resurrection Life

Blessed be the God and Father of our Lord Jesus Christ, who according to His great mercy has caused us to be born again to a living hope through the resurrection of Jesus Christ from the dead.

1 PETER 1:3 NASB

God, in his great mercy, has always intended for us to be alive in his love. In the communion of fellowship with him, we find that he is full of compassion. His kindness is unmatched. When Jesus rose from the grave and defeated death, it was with the same power of God that we have through the Spirit.

Resurrection life is ours through Christ; just as he was raised from death to life, so are we—both in eternity and here in this life. He tore down every barrier that would keep us from the abundance of his love. Where we see lack in our lives is an invitation to see God's power at work. When we align our lives with him, we can be sure that he will turn our mourning into gladness and our sorrow into joy!

Holy One, your mercy is beyond my understanding. Open the eyes of my heart to see your power at work in my life right here and now. Spirit, may you breathe your life into my weary soul once again and wake me up. I honor you as I cling to you.

Thoughts of Peace

"I know the thoughts that I think toward you,"
says the LORD,
"thoughts of peace and not of evil,
to give you a future and a hope."

JEREMIAH 29:11 NKJV

God's ways are better than our ways and his thoughts are above ours. His intentions toward us are good—full of peace and kindness. The Lord does not wish us harm, and he does not plan our destruction.

If your thoughts are not filled with peace about your circumstances or about yourself, you can rest assured that they are not God's thoughts toward you. You may be feeling the chaos of worry about the future, but God is not worried. His plans always include mercy, love, and hope. If you are struggling to feel hope for your future, ask God for his perspective of your life.

Lord, your Word says that your thoughts toward me are full of peace. I ask for fresh revelation today to know the clear difference between your voice and my own. You are always better than I am, so I trust you to help me and breathe hope into me again. Thank you for your endless kindness, Lord.

Great Confidence

*He's the hope that holds me
and the Stronghold to shelter me,
the only God for me,
and my great confidence.*

PSALM 91:2 TPT

There is not much in this life that is absolutely stable. Economies fluctuate, families break apart, and the weather is increasingly unpredictable. What we can be sure of is that though changes happen outside of our control, God is always a shelter to take refuge in. He never changes; he is not like the shifting winds.

When you feel the weight of uncertainty threatening your peace, remember that God is the hope that holds you. Everything else is but a detail, and he is more detail oriented than you could ever be. Let God be the safe place where you run, finding your confidence in his incomparable goodness. He will not let you down.

God, you are my greatest treasure. Everything I could ever need and more is found in you. Where my mind has been swirling from the unknown and stresses of life, breathe your peace. You're the only God for me. May I be full of confidence when I consider your greatness.

Answered

By awesome deeds you answer us with deliverance,
O God of our salvation;
you are the hope of all the ends of the earth
and of the farthest seas.

PSALM 65:5 NRSV

We cannot escape the shadows of this world, where trials come in many different forms. We may be faced with sickness, depression, grief, or failure, but that is not our end. God is the hope of all the ends of the earth; he is our hope.

Just as God delivered the Israelites out of the hand of Egypt, so will he deliver you. Whatever dark season you are walking through is not the end of your story. He will come through for you and lead you into freedom again. The sun will rise, and the light of God will make all that is hidden clear as day. Wait for him; he will answer you.

Yahweh, you are my salvation. I believe that you have not abandoned me to the darkness of my circumstances. Shine your light on my life and lead me into your joy! I lift my eyes to you again, Lord, my hope and my deliverer.

Guided by Truth

Guide me in your truth and teach me,
for you are God my Savior,
and my hope is in you all day long.

PSALM 25:5 NIV

God is not a tyrant, and he is not demanding. He is an amazing leader and the best teacher we could ever find. The Holy Spirit is our constant companion, leading us into all truth. What an amazing gift we've been given in God's presence, which is always with us. What incredible hope that he has given us instructions in his Word that guide us.

When we look at the way of love, which is the way that the Lord leads us, we can be encouraged that everything we are learning and doing in this life is covered by grace. We don't need to get it right to be righteous—he's already done that work for us. There is room in his love to make mistakes as we learn to walk in his way. As we keep our hearts humble before him, we are able to keep growing as his children.

Lord, you are so gracious in the way you lead. Help me to remember that you correct with kindness and you direct with love. I want to be just like you. I know that your way is better than my own. Guide me, God; you are where all my hope lies.

Believe

*To all who did accept him and believe in him
he gave the right to become children of God.*

JOHN 1:12 NCV

The eyes of faith help us cling to what is beyond our natural vision. God is not a man that he should lie, nor do his intentions change. As he was at the beginning, so he will always be. Where we have a wrong understanding of his character and nature, may our hearts be molded by the love that meets us in our humility.

Belief is not a blind action, ignoring the reality around us. We can believe in God and also bring him every question, every wondering, and every hesitation. As children of God, we have the relationship of family to approach him with every shallow and deep thought. He leads us, nurtures us, and corrects us in kindness. How could we be unchanged by such an exchange?

Father, I come to you today as a dearly loved child, knowing I do not need to hold anything back from you. In vulnerability, I approach you with my longings, questions, and my devotion. Knowing I am loved and accepted by you fills my heart with the confidence that with you I can face anything.

Not Afraid

"This is my command—be strong and courageous!
Do not be afraid or discouraged.
For the LORD your God is with you wherever you go."
JOSHUA 1:9 NLT

There is no doubt that we face many tests in this life. There is no way to avoid trials and troubles, though they look different for each of us. God is with us in whatever circumstance arises. There is nothing too difficult for him, and he will never look at us, or our situations, and decide it is too much for him to be invested in.

There is a reason that the Word encourages us to be strong and courageous! What does courage look like? In the face of fear, it is perseverance. In the face of discouragement, it is refusing to give up hope, even if it feels like the smallest sliver. May we be able to join with those who have gone before us, fighting the good fight, keeping the faith, and finishing the race.

Lord my God, I take courage in your Word that says you are with me wherever I go. When fear threatens to immobilize me, I will abide in you, allowing your presence to empower me with what I cannot conjure up on my own. You are life to my soul, breath to my lungs, and refreshing water that washes over me. You are my God, and I am yours!

Eyes Opened

I pray that the eyes of your heart may be enlightened,
so that you will know what is the hope of His calling,
what are the riches of the glory of His inheritance in the saints.

EPHESIANS 1:18 NASB

Have you ever had a lightbulb moment? A profound moment of realization about something that was once hidden to you? That is what revelation is. Consider when you first believed that Jesus was the Son of God. What captivated you about him?

There is no end to the revelations of God's character in our lives. There is always more. He is infinitely better than we can ever imagine him to be. Today, may the prayer of Paul to the Ephesians pave the way for the eyes of our own hearts to be enlightened by the glorious reality of God's goodness. He is full of unending wonders to discover!

Glorious King, illuminate the eyes of my heart to see the wonder of who you are in a new way today. May I see clearly the way you physically provide for your children. May my imagination be filled with the glory of your light alive in me. You are so good, Lord!

Real Revelation

Your faith and love rise within you as you access all the treasures of your inheritance stored up in the heavenly realm. For the revelation of the true gospel is as real today as the day you first heard of our glorious hope, now that you have believed in the truth of the gospel.

COLOSSIANS 1:5 TPT

There is a rich beauty in understanding the gospel of Jesus Christ, the fruit of which is that souls are won over by love. There is freedom to come alive in the affection that has led us back to the arms of our good Father.

We are not bound by duty; God is not a slave driver, requiring more of us than we can give and working us to the bone. He is a loving leader who calls us to a better way—the path of love. Jesus showed us the way to live, love, and lead in the way he poured out his own life. He doesn't require perfection from us; he takes our willing, open hearts and as we live out love, we find that we are continually filled with more, straight from his heart. Let faith arise today.

Glorious God, thank you for the mystery of the gospel that fills me with hope to live out of the generosity of your heart. Truly everything you do is done out of deep affection. Where there is resistance to this within my heart, I ask for fresh revelation to receive your abundant love. May faith arise within me today.

Anchor of the Soul

This hope we have as an anchor of the soul,
both sure and steadfast,
and which enters the Presence behind the veil.

HEBREWS 6:19 NKJV

Through the faithfulness of God to his own Word and intentions, our souls have been anchored to the King of heaven and earth. Our hope is not dependent on ourselves or our own feeble belief. Our hope is sure, never shaken, because it is based on the loyalty of the Holy One who never fails.

This anchor of the soul keeps us from drifting with the shifting tides and winds. Even when storms come, we will be held secure. May our hearts find confidence in the one who holds us steady. He is faithful to do everything that he set out to do. When we struggle to see purpose in our lives and can't see how things will ever work together, let us remember that even when we cannot see, God knows the bigger picture and he is not done with us yet!

Holy One, you are faithful. You keep me firmly planted in your love. Thank you for never letting go of me no matter what happens in this life. I trust you even as confusion crops up. You are better than I am, and I know that I will see your hand of mercy on every area of my life.

June

"Don't let your hearts be troubled.
Trust in God, and trust also in me."

JOHN 14:1 NLT

Endurance

Love bears all things,
believes all things,
hopes all things,
endures all things.

1 CORINTHIANS 13:7 ESV

The very character of God is love. Jesus bore and endured everything that came his way. He believed and hoped through every circumstance. When we do the same, we are reflecting the nature of God who is alive within us. He is able to do immeasurably more than we could ever ask or imagine. Why would we not trust him?

As we endure the hard circumstances of life, God's grace strengthens us. We are not left to do any of it on our own. We have access to the same Spirit who empowered Jesus to rise from the grave! If death truly was defeated, then anything that we face is certainly covered by the same overcoming power. Hold on; he is not done with you yet.

Compassionate One, you are the one I hold onto throughout my life. I cannot let you go, and even if I did, you would not let go of me. Fill me with your tangible love that strengthens and empowers me to live as Jesus did. You are worth it all!

Heartsick

Hope deferred makes the heart sick,
But desire fulfilled is a tree of life.

PROVERBS 13:12 NASB

Longings of the heart are not small matters. When promises are delayed and we are in the waiting, it can be hard to keep believing in hope. Our hearts break as we struggle with disappointment. But God is not cruel. Even as we wait, he is present with us in the heartbreak and the longing.

As you wait on your delayed desires, find your comfort in the arms of your loving God. He is no consolation prize—he is the ultimate goal. He is better than the gifts you are waiting on. They reveal his character; they are glimpses of the enormity of his goodness and glory. Take heart, he who is with you is the fulfillment of every longing you could ever have.

Lord over all, you are the answer to every longing I have. What I think is good is just a glimpse of something even better—you! Fill my heart with hunger for fellowship with you as you reveal yourself through the gifts you give. I know that you are really what I long for.

Steadfast Hope

The Lord takes pleasure in those who fear him,
in those who hope in his steadfast love.
PSALM 147:11 NRSV

The love of God is steadier than the largest mountain on earth. He will not be swayed away from compassion or mercy—it is who he is. In the same way, we find hope in this unending, unmoving, fiery love. When all seems lost, let us lift our eyes to our lover God who never changes his mind about us.

Hope does not always come easily; it is like warfare to anticipate God's goodness in the face of trials and circumstances that test our belief systems. When it comes down to it, our confidence is not based on our own works or worth; it is based on the God who never changes. Take hope in him today.

Lord, you are where all my hopes find their fulfillment. You are the hand that steadies me throughout my life. Help me to stay close to you. I am yours for all my days. Meet me in the middle of my mess, Lord, and fill my heart with your peace.

Hurry to Help

God, hurry to help me, run to my rescue!
For you're my Savior and my only hope!
PSALM 38:22 TPT

There are times in life that we are desperate for God's intervention. There is no other way to describe our need than absolute dependency on the miracle maker. When we are solely reliant on heaven's involvement to change our situation, it can feel like we're grasping at the air. But this is not the case.

God is a rescuer, an ever-present help in times of trouble. Cry out to God from the depths of your soul and watch as he comes to your aid. He will do it because he is faithful. The God of angel armies is the same God who saves you. Wait on him. He will not delay!

Savior, I need your help more than I can express. When my heart starts to quake with fear, I turn to you. Hear me and save me! You are the solid support I need and my only hope.

Yes and Amen

*All of God's promises have been fulfilled in Christ
with a resounding "Yes!"*

2 CORINTHIANS 1:20 NLT

The promises of God do not depend on our abilities to accomplish them. They belong to the Lord and are sealed by his faithfulness. Though we falter in faith, God never wavers in dependability. He is the same yesterday, today, and forever. All of his ways are just and true. Though the seasons shift and everything changes, he is the steady foundation, our unshakeable hope, who never ever varies.

Where you have felt your hope start to fade, press into the character of God. Stir up your history with God and be reminded of his loyal love to all who call on his name. He does not change his mind. You are his, surrounded by his peace and full of his mercy. Reach out today; you will not be disappointed in the presence of God.

Faithful One, your loyal love is the sustenance of my soul. When I am depleted of hope and any strength to keep going, I know that you are more than enough for me. Holy Spirit, fill me as I wait on you. Encourage my heart today in your kindness.

Brave Enough

On the day I called you, you answered me.
You made me strong and brave.

PSALM 138:3 NCV

God is always ready to answer the cries of those who call out to him. He does not delay. He doesn't try to prove a point in silence or feed our insecurity by making us wait. Even in the waiting, we find that the fullness of his presence is our portion. He does not give sparingly; he always offers the abundance of his heart.

When circumstances have us unsure of the outcome, we can find our rest and security in the character of God. We find courage in the loyal love of our good and faithful Father. In him, we find the strength we need. He will not fail us, and he will not betray us. The nature of God is always compassionate, merciful, and generous.

Steady One, you are the rock I stand upon. Today, I call on you, and I trust that you will answer me. Meet me with the power of your presence. In my weakness, be my strength and encourage my heart. You make me brave.

Wonderful Things

Lord, you are my God;
I will exalt you and praise your name,
for in perfect faithfulness
you have done wonderful things,
things planned long ago.

ISAIAH 25:1 NIV

God's ways are full of wisdom. He sees the big picture as well as every detail. He is not reckless in the ways he moves, and he is not distant. He works in perfect faithfulness, always following through. He does not forget his promises, and he does not grow weary of fulfilling any of them.

Where we struggle to see the goodness in our lives, let us look to the character of our good Father. Has he forgotten anything? Has he left any detail untouched? In his mercy, he meets us right where we are, but he does not leave us there. He picks us up and leads us on in his perfect love. Let our hearts take hope in his faithfulness.

Lord, you are my God. You are the one I depend on in every circumstance. In your perfect faithfulness, meet me and fulfill every one of your promises in wonderful ways. You are so, so good!

Wait on the Lord

*It is good that one should hope
and wait quietly for the salvation of the LORD.*

LAMENTATIONS 3:26 NKJV

When the chaos of our lives won't relent and the anxieties in our minds prevent us from resting, let us take the time to quiet our hearts in God's presence. Sometimes this will look like intentionally crying out to God for help; other times, it will be taking a few minutes in a quiet place to breathe deeply and slowly.

The salvation of the Lord is always at hand. He does not abandon us to the overwhelming despair that comes from uncontrollable situations. When sorrow, pain, and suffering are unavoidable, God shows up in the power of his presence to sustain, comfort, and carry us. He is our best and truest hope. In him, nothing goes wasted. Not even the darkest night. In the waiting, he is there.

Loyal God, you consistently show up to save me. You are not a one-time help in times of trouble—you are always available, and you never hesitate to show up. I need you today. Calm the anxieties of my heart as I look to you. Meet me with the power of your presence, bringing peace to the chaos.

Do Not Forget

You have forgotten that Yahweh, your Maker,
stretched out the skies and laid earth's firm foundation.
But you live each day constantly worrying,
living in fear of your angry oppressor
who is bent on your destruction.
But their fury cannot touch you!

ISAIAH 51:13 TPT

How convinced are we that God will keep us safe? When we feel defeated and overcome by failure or overwhelming circumstances outside of our control, do we succumb to worry, or do we turn our hearts in trust to our defender and Savior? His power has not diminished over time and his heart of love has not changed.

The maker of heaven and earth is our Father. He does not abandon us to destruction. In his faithful love, he protects us and guides us. He is our deliverer. He will not feed us to the wolves or let us be overcome by those who seek to humiliate us. He is so much better than that. We are hidden in his love, and he will sustain us through every trying circumstance.

Yahweh, you are all powerful. Your love is the strongest force in the universe, and I am completely covered in it. I will take hope in you again today, turning my eyes to you every time I am overcome by the worries of life. You are above them all and you are faithful to deliver me.

Provision Is Yours

*"Do not worry then, saying,
'What will we eat?'
or 'What will we drink?'
or 'What will we wear for clothing?'"*

MATTHEW 6:31 NASB

In God we have access to everything we need. When we don't know how we will get by or get through, God miraculously provides for our needs. He is not slow to save or delayed in his response to us. When the Israelites wandered the desert before entering the Promised Land, they were fed straight from heaven each morning. The manna they received was incredibly provided, and they didn't even need to ask.

In the same way, we can trust that God will supply everything we need. We don't need to beg him to give us what we need to survive. He does it out of the goodness of his faithful heart. His track record of provision is perfect. Why then do we worry about the essentials of our lives being met? It is all delivered from God's abundant storehouse. He always has more than enough. We will not go without.

Provider, I remember again today that everything I need is offered from your generous heart. I will not go without the sustenance I need; worry is just wasted effort. Fill me with the peace and confidence that comes from your nearness. You are everything I need.

Always Gracious

The LORD always keeps his promises;
he is gracious in all he does.

PSALM 145:13 NLT

When we consider the faithfulness of God, where is there room to doubt his goodness toward us? But even if we do, it does not affect his loyal character. We cannot jinx his mercy; we cannot affect his integrity. He stands alone in compassion, always giving it out of his generous heart.

The Lord does not go back on his Word, and we cannot talk him out of his intentions. In everything he does, he is full of mercy. His grace is given freely in every circumstance, fueling us with his strength. Where we lack, he has more than enough. He is benevolent and kind, always considerate and gentle in the ways that he deals with us. We don't need to fear punishment or retribution in his presence. As we experience his caring, we grow more confident and loving ourselves.

Gracious God, I can't begin to thank you for your generosity toward me. You never fail to reach out in love, and you don't leave me dry. Your mercy is my life-blood—it strengthens me. I rely on you today. You are faithful.

Safe Place

The Lord is good,
a refuge in times of trouble.
He cares for those who trust in him.

NAHUM 1:7 NIV

All those who come to God for shelter from the storms of life will find rest in his arms. He is a caring Father who always supplies what his children need. His comfort is unmatched; it's even better than the most empathetic mother in the world. His character is good, and he will never let us down.

When you consider trusting God with the outcomes of situations in your life, what feeling does this evoke? Do you find comfort in God being in control, or does it stir up even more anxiety? Where there are doubts about God's goodness, let it take you to his feet in conversation. He can handle every question you have. Let today be the day you lay it all bare before him. Don't hold back!

Lord, here I am with all of my questions and my doubts. Here I am with my feeble trust. I want to know the confidence of faith in your good character. I believe that you are my best option even when I struggle to hope in your love. Holy Spirit, override my mind with your perfect peace. Encounter me with your presence today.

Fully Equipped

*All scripture is inspired by God and is useful for teaching, for reproof,
for correction, and for training in righteousness, so that everyone who
belongs to God may be proficient, equipped for every good work.*

2 Timothy 3:16-17 NRSV

Where there is lack of trust in God, there is a gap in understanding of his perfect nature. We will find everything we could ever need—every resource, all the strength we require—within the presence of our good God. In his Word, we find keys to living a life that is full of the fruit of the Spirit. As yielded ones, we submit our hearts to God's wisdom and follow in the path of love he has paved.

Where you have need, God has provision. Where you have questions, God holds answers and solutions. He is so much better than our best teachers. There is no problem that can confound him. There is no mountain that he cannot move. He is perfect in power, in wisdom, and in compassion. There is none like him.

Good God, I am so indebted to your faithfulness. Where I have struggled to see your love at work in my life, open my eyes to your perspective. Even as I struggle, I hold onto hope that you really are all I need. Come through for me, Lord!

Listen Closely

My child, pay attention to my words;
listen closely to what I say.
Don't ever forget my words;
keep them always in mind.

PROVERBS 4:20-21 NCV

In the craziness of life, slowing down and paying attention to details can seem overwhelming. When God speaks, he does so in the gentle whisper of love and mercy. He is kind, and often it is kindness that we overlook. When someone acts uncharacteristically generous, doesn't it fill us with wonder?

For God, generosity is his signature. He is full of compassion to all who come to him. If someone is claiming to speak on behalf of God, and what they're saying is not laced with love, we must question the source. When we consider God's unchanging character, we can listen closely for his whisper in our lives and find that he is there. He is present with us. His love never lets go!

Father God, you are the author of mercy, full of lovingkindness. When I look in your Word, I find that you continually met people with the goodness of your character. Knowing that you don't change, I am full of hope that you will also meet me with the kindness of your presence! Reveal yourself in a new way today, Lord.

Rightful Pursuit

*Whoever pursues righteousness and love
finds life, prosperity and honor.*
PROVERBS 21:21 NIV

God is light, and in him everything is brought to light. He makes the most muddled situations clear with the precision of his perspective. As we pursue God's good nature in our lives, we will find the life and honor we are looking for. We will find all the fullness we seek in the virtues of our God and King.

As we worship God, we begin to understand that he is better than any expression of love we encounter on this earth. He is purer than our highest morals. He has no hidden motives, and as we are filled by his revelation light, we find that we need not. Our loving response to living submitted to his heart is a natural response to the unfiltered worth we find in being loved by the King of kings.

Merciful King, you are above all and yet you are concerned with every little detail. Nothing escapes your notice, least of all me! As you fill me with the liquid love of your presence, I am empowered to love you and others in return. Your ways are so much better than any I've ever known. Thank you for life.

Hiding Place

You are my hiding place;
You shall preserve me from trouble;
You shall surround me with songs of deliverance.

PSALM 32:7 NKJV

When troubles overtake us and we are overwhelmed by the demands of life, where do we turn? God is a safe place to find refuge. He never turns us away when we look to him. He keeps us secure in the covering of his love. We can never go outside of the confines of his kindness and compassion.

When we feel exposed by our fear, God shields us in his great affection. He cannot be convinced out of his mercy. It's not within the realm of possibility because God is love. When we feel completely out of our depth, we can be sure that God is never overwhelmed. He is full of wisdom when we need it. His love never fails!

God, you are my hiding place. I run to you in my fear—when I am overwhelmed, you come in with your perfect peace and cover me. I don't want to venture out on my own; I rely on you today and every day.

My Only Hope

It is through him that you now believe in God,
who raised him from the dead and glorified him,
so that you would fasten your faith and hope in God alone.

1 PETER 1:21 TPT

Jesus is the purest example of God's love to us. Jesus, the Son of God and Son of Man, embodied relationship with the Father and the expression of his compassion to all. It is through him that we are given access to the same kind of close relationship with our good Father. He never fails and is perfect in his parenting. We need never fear hidden motives lurking within his heart because he is pure, transparent love.

When our expectations in life are disappointed and our plans fall apart, what do we do? Failure is inevitable, and setbacks are par for the course. There is no perfect life; but God's mercy is full of amazing fruit. He takes the ashes of our circumstances and somehow makes something sweet grow out of them. His plans are better than any we could make. As we stay connected to him, we will find that he orchestrates a beautiful medley out of what sounds strange in isolation. He is blending the pieces of our lives together even now.

God, you are my hope. Take my life and make it something beautiful. I trust you to lead me into life; you are so good.

United Heart

Teach me your way, O LORD,
that I may walk in your truth;
unite my heart to fear your name.

PSALM 86:11 ESV

Where our hearts are divided, there is competition for control. When we follow the Lord, walking in his truth, we submit our hearts wholly to him. We lead ourselves into his presence and he leads us into life. There is no better guide in this existence. The author of time and space is the one who directs our steps.

Are our hearts completely his? If not, we should consider allowing him into the whole of them. It is natural to have parts of us that distrust even God, but that does not mean we cannot invite the Spirit to minister wholeness to every part of our beings. As we welcome God's presence to bring restoration and unity within us, we submit ourselves to his goodness. He is tender and kind.

Lord, you are the kindest healer there is. You mend with compassion. How could I not trust your goodness? Especially where I struggle, you are welcome to speak your words of restoration life. You are better than I am, and I know I can rely on you to make me whole.

In the Meantime

*Training us to…live lives that are self-controlled, upright, and godly,
while we wait for the blessed hope and the manifestation of the glory
of our great God and Savior, Jesus Christ.*

TITUS 2:12-13 NRSV

In this life, waiting is a given. Patience is not, however. Endurance is conditioned with intentionality and practice. As we yield to God's ways, we are constantly being trained in his character. We get to train in his nature so that we reflect him. He is full of wisdom that is clear minded. He is righteous in all his ways; his intentions and actions do not change based on different people or locales. He is pure in love, never withholding compassion from any who seek it.

In the same way, our lives will bear the fruit of God's kingdom as we practice being peaceful and kind. As we forgive those whom others hate, we exhibit God's mercy. When we choose to meet others in their suffering, we practice the same kind of comfort we receive from the Father. As we wait for Jesus' return, we can clearly see God's children through his goodness exhibited in their lives.

God, I want to live a life that reflects your amazing character—full of compassion, kindness, tender mercy, and wisdom. It is not a chore to be loved by you, and though it is not easy to live that same kind of love, it is so worth it to choose it!

Run to Safety

The name of the LORD is a strong tower;
the righteous runs into it and is safe.

PROVERBS 18:10 NASB

There is a lot that threatens our peace throughout the day. Whether it's physical, spiritual, or emotional, we face crises that drain our strength and resources. We only have so much to give, and when it's gone, what then? When we are depleted of our own means to get by, may we run into the shelter of the Most High.

Where God is, there is hope. He covers us with his compassion as we run to him. He is our place of safety and refuge; he is not intimidated by the struggles we face. When arrows fly toward us, he wraps around us, and the arrows are absorbed by his tender mercy. He will not let us fall, and he won't let us be overtaken. He is faithful!

Lord, you are the place I find reprieve and rest from the storms of life. I look for comfort around me, but I only find true consolation in you. May the power of your presence surround me as I run toward you. Be my shield and my defender.

All I Need

The Lord is all I need.
He takes care of me.
My share in life has been pleasant;
my part has been beautiful.

PSALM 16:5-6 NCV

When we feel isolated and alone, everything seems harder. We were simply not meant to carry ourselves through this life by sheer willpower. We need help, and we require community to thrive. Leaning on others in our weakness is not a fault; it is a strength!

When we have no one around us who understands what we are going through, especially in suffering, the weight of pain can feel especially heavy. But there is one who understands. God, our comforter, is with us in the most soul-crushing agony of our hearts. He does not write off our suffering, but he does meet us in the midst of it with his mercy and power. He takes care of us and turns our ashes into beauty every time.

Lord, you are all I need. When I feel alone in my sadness, meet me in the middle of it with your unfailing love. Strengthen me and hold me up. I am so grateful that you take care of me perfectly. Surround me with your presence and put people as supports in my life as well.

Generous Living

"Give, and it will be given to you. A good measure, pressed down,
shaken together and running over, will be poured into your lap.
For with the measure you use, it will be measured to you."
LUKE 6:38 NIV

The heart of God is abundant in nature. It cannot be held in; it would surely burst at the seams if we attempted to contain it. When we live with generosity as a value, we reflect God's character. Not only that, but when we give out of the willingness of our hearts, we will be filled in the same measure.

There is no lack in God's heart, and we don't need to worry about exhausting his resources. With access to the source of all life, we can freely live out the same generosity that is liberally given to us with no concern of running out. Where we have need, we can be sure that God will meet it. We don't have to be anxious about his provision.

Gracious God, you generously give to all who come to you. As you fill my life with everything I need, may I in turn be liberal in love to those around me. Give me confidence as I rest in your presence.

Never Disappointed

Here's what I've learned through it all:
Don't give up; don't be impatient;
be entwined as one with the Lord.
Be brave and courageous, and never lose hope.
Yes, keep on waiting—for he will never disappoint you!
PSALM 27:14 TPT

Our timing is not the same as God's timing. When we're waiting, it can feel discouraging if we are doing it on our own with no end in sight. But when we actively connect with the Lord in the delay, we will find that his faithful character sustains us. He is our source of courage—not our own tenacity.

When we are tempted to give up, let us not let go of hope altogether. As we remain knit into God's presence, we will find grace to continue to wait. Though circumstances may disappoint, he never will. His nature is faithfulness, and we can rely on his goodness to be present every step of the journey.

Faithful One, you never let me go. Even as I falter in faith, you hold on tight. Give me courage to continue to press into you in the waiting and to trust that you will never go back on your promises. You are so good, God!

Coming Joy

The hope of the righteous ends in gladness,
but the expectation of the wicked comes to nothing.

PROVERBS 10:28 NRSV

It is a good, if painful, practice to exercise awareness of where our expectations lie. What are we expecting of those closest to us? How about ourselves? And God? It is too simplistic to say that there are few, for we have many underlying hopes that we may not even be aware of. Even so, there are probably some close to the surface for us today.

Not all anticipation is equal. It is not all based on truth. It is important to know what our hearts are hoping for in order to understand the source and the projection. In God's Word, he has laid out his love in terms that are simple. When we live according to God's way of mercy, we will find that the hope of God's love accomplishing all it has set out to do will be fulfilled.

Lord, you are the joy of my heart, and I know that I will be full of gladness when you come through on your promises. Help me to know your ways and your wisdom as I walk this world with you. I align myself to your heart as I lean into you for strength today.

Strength to go On

I can do everything through Christ,
who gives me strength.
PHILIPPIANS 4:13 NLT

In the trials and the changes of life, we are not left to fend for ourselves. We need not rely on our own abilities, power, and resources alone to get through. In fact, it is in our weakness that God becomes our strength. He has an endless supply of power that is always accessible through his mercy and love.

In his presence, we are saturated with his kindness and compassion. It refreshes us and brings us life. Where we are depleted, the Spirit floods us with God's unrelenting love that fuels us to do everything that we must. He is the fire to our furnace, the gas in our tank, and every motivation we need. In Christ, we truly can do all things because he is the source of everything we require.

God, all my strength comes from you. My resources are quickly depleted, but in you I find what I need to go on. I lean into your love and you fill me with the power of your presence. What else could I require?

Fought For

*The Lord your God is the one who goes with you
to fight for you against your enemies to give you victory.*

DEUTERONOMY 20:4 NIV

Some battles in our lives are just too much for us to face on our own. In every struggle, we have one who goes with us to fight for us. He is the triumphant one who prevails every time. There is not a situation that is too difficult that God cannot turn it around. He can take even the most desolate circumstance and bring life out of it.

What are you facing in your life right now that seems too much to handle? Even this is not too complicated for the Lord. He is your sustainer, your defender, and your deliverer. He goes with you into every situation; he is with you now, and he will be with you when you need him. He will not withdraw and leave you on your own. Lean into his strength and you will find that there is more than enough grace to sustain you.

Defender, you are constantly with me. I am so grateful that I am not left to fight for myself. When I am overcome by harsh realities, you take care of me in your lovingkindness. Who can stand against your mercy?

Sustained by Love

Sustain me according to Your word, that I may live;
And do not let me be ashamed of my hope.

PSALM 119:116 NASB

When the storms of life toss us around, it can be difficult to find our grounding. Where is God in this? We might ask. We may find it hard to see his goodness at all. But even in the chaos, God is full of peace. His Word calms the wildest tempest and makes the sea like glass.

God's Word is full of light; it is sustenance for those who are hungry. We will not be ashamed of our hope if our hope is in God and his faithfulness. When we wonder whether he is present, let us look into history to see what it reveals about his character. When we look with eyes of faith, we will see him. His goodness is inescapable, and his mercy cannot be exaggerated. What a wonderful love that sustains us!

Lord, you are the one who holds my life. You keep me even as I stumble. Lord, be the strength of my heart and the wisdom that I so desperately need. I depend on you to come through, and I believe that you will.

Healing on the Horizon

For you who fear my name,
the sun of righteousness shall rise
with healing in its wings.

MALACHI 4:2 ESV

As we live our lives yielded to the Son of God, we are covered by his wonderful love. When Jesus walked the earth, he didn't just heal a few but all of the sick who came to him. He never turned them away. In the same way, he does not turn us away when we come to him.

Where in your body or your life do you need healing? Do you trust that the one who healed the sick and raised the dead will do the same for you today? He is more skilled than the most trusted doctor, and he knows you inside out. Come to him with your pain today; he is the healer, and he will meet you.

Healer, touch me with your mercy today. Bring everything that is out of alignment with you and your kingdom back into alignment with your purposes and intentions in Jesus' name. You are incredibly kind and good, and I will not hold back from asking you. Restore me, Lord, and heal me today.

Thoughtful Living

Don't act thoughtlessly,
but understand what the Lord wants you to do.
EPHESIANS 5:17 NLT

Wisdom is found in the Lord. He is full of insight; his Word is an incredible guide to understanding his nature that is full of mercy and kindness. When we look for wisdom, God's Word says that we will find it. It is compared to the most incredible treasure that can be found, worth more than rubies or gold.

When we seek to know God in relationship, we find that he is better than we could have ever imagined. His love never lets go and his faithfulness knows no end. When we consider his attributes, we discover that to live like him means to consider others in greater measure than we consider our own desires. Thoughtful living doesn't mean to be a martyr, but it does require sacrifice.

Lord, I need more of your wisdom in my life. Help me to see from your perspective and to understand how it is you want me to live. I don't want to mindlessly live according to my whims. Empower me to live with purpose and mercy as my covering.

A Place Prepared

"Let not your heart be troubled; you believe in God, believe also in Me. In My Father's house are many mansions. I go to prepare a place for you. And if I go and prepare a place for you, I will come again and receive you to Myself; that where I am, there you may be also."

JOHN 14:1-3 NKJV

In a fast-paced world where life changes frequently and quickly, may we not lose sight of the long-lasting values that remain unaltered. Jesus did not come to pacify the wealthy and stroke the egos of the powerful; he came to heal and save those who were needy and lost. His love is boundless and knows no measure. It can't be bought or sold. He gives freely to all who would receive.

Jesus has prepared a place for all of those he came to save. You are included in this. If you are struggling to believe today, let your heart be open to God's faithfulness. He has not failed yet, and he won't start now. Don't be troubled by the timeline; God is still working!

Lord, strengthen my heart to trust you. I don't want to be overwhelmed by worries, and that is a real possibility. Flood my mind with your peace, my heart with your love, and my body with healing. Do what only you can do and make the wrong things right. Redeemer, show up and show off.

July

Give all your worries to him,
because he cares about you.

1 PETER 5:7 NCV

Champion Defender

He alone is my safe place;
his wrap-around presence always protects me.
For he is my champion defender;
there's no risk of failure with God.
So why would I let worry paralyze me,
even when troubles multiply around me?

PSALM 62:2 TPT

When troubles increase in our lives, it can be difficult to not be overcome with worry. God is described as a safe place; he is fully present with us, protecting us with the covering of his always-available love. He never fails. As we wait on him, we let our hearts take courage in this truth!

Where you are overwhelmed by the distress of your circumstances, turn your attention to the faithfulness of God. As David poured out his heart to God in the psalms, you too can pour out every emotion, every longing, every hope, and every disappointment as you experience it. Stir up your history with God and see through the lens of his constant faithfulness in your life. Where you cannot see him, trust that he will give you eyes to see where his deliverance is along the way.

Defender, you are the only one I can truly rely on. Where I fall short, where others fail me, you remain constant and faithful. I will not forget what you have done for me. Lord, stir up hope that I would trust you to continue to be present with me in every trouble I face.

Home in Him

A father of the fatherless and a judge for the widows,
is God in His holy habitation.
God makes a home for the lonely;
He leads out the prisoners into prosperity.

PSALM 68:5-6 NASB

When you think of home, what does that image evoke in you? Is it a place of rest and safety? Comfort and peace? Or is your definition of home unstable and chaotic? Whatever your experience of home as a child, you can be sure that God's household is a place of peace, tranquility, and ease. In his house, you are completely welcome to be you—no pretending, no self-protecting—just you.

God is a father to the fatherless; he sets the lonely in community. We are united in God's family. As children of God, we have space to grow and the freedom to grow up in him. Where we have felt isolated and on the outside, God has welcomed us in. We belong to him. We belong in him. We belong.

God, you are my place of refuge and safety. You are my home. Lead me into peace as I find my rest in your presence. Teach me and guide me; love me to life again today.

Confident Help

We can say with confidence,
"The LORD is my helper, so I will have no fear.
What can mere people do to me?"
HEBREWS 13:6 NLT

Life is full of unexpected turns. We cannot avoid change, nor can we predict what our lives will look like in one year or ten. We cannot control whether others will accept or reject us. When it comes to our expectations, we can be sure that reality will often look vastly different.

So, what then? Do we throw up our hands in surrender? Well, yes. That is exactly how we can respond. God who is unchanging in his love and wisdom is never surprised by anything. We do not surrender to our circumstances and to fear; we surrender to the wisdom and leadership of God through it all. Our confidence is in God, and he is always ready to help us when we need it.

Lord, my heart takes courage in your consistent love. You do not change from day to day. You are the same powerful, merciful God that you have always been and will always be. Redirect my gaze to your goodness when I am tempted to be overcome by shifting circumstances. I surrender to your ways, Lord, knowing your wisdom is better than the world's ways!

Restored by Rest

The LORD is my shepherd, I shall not want.
He makes me lie down in green pastures;
he leads me beside still waters; he restores my soul.

PSALM 23:1-3 NRSV

Left to our own whims and desires, we wander from thing to thing like sheep left to meander on their own. We can easily lose our way and find that we have drifted from what was familiar and safe into the wild unknown. The Lord is a faithful shepherd who finds us and leads us to a place of rest for our souls. He always knows the best way out of the chaos we find ourselves in.

God is a faithful protector, guarding us from the enemy that is waiting for an opportunity to destroy us. Our good leader is a place of refuge, and he keeps a watchful eye on us. He gives us everything we need. He is the perfect provider. Best of all, he never gives up on us. He is constantly pursuing us in love.

Good Shepherd, I am so grateful to be yours. You lead me along the path you have prepared for me. As I follow you, you bring me to places of rest where you refresh me. I trust your leadership in my life. Thank you for never giving up on me.

He Is Near

The LORD is near to the brokenhearted
and saves the crushed in spirit.
PSALM 34:18 ESV

It is not a failure to be heartbroken and discouraged. Troubles in life are inevitable; they touch us all. We do not reflect the heart of our Father when we ignore suffering whether that of others or our own. When pain is overwhelming and we struggle to hope for anything better, God is close.

May today be the day you sense the nearness of God in indescribable measure. He does not command you to be happy; he draws close to the brokenhearted and saves those whose spirits are discouraged. His comfort is yours here and now. You are not alone. May you see how close he is even in this present moment.

Lord, you are incredible in how you are drawn to the humble and the broken. I will not hide my face from you today. Come closer than my very breath. Fill me with the comfort of your presence. You're all I have.

Guarded by Wisdom

Wisdom will come into your mind,
and knowledge will be pleasing to you.
Good sense will protect you;
understanding will guard you.
It will keep you from the wicked,
from those whose words are bad.
PROVERBS 2:10-12 NCV

Wisdom is not a vain pursuit. We may spend our time increasing our knowledge in various ways, but true wisdom is found in God. In his Word, we find keys to living in the light of wisdom. A good starting place is to look at the life of Jesus. He is wisdom embodied.

Where in life do you need understanding? Human insight only goes so far. Will you lean into the Lord and ask for his perception over your circumstances? He has the answers and solutions for each problem that arises. You can trust him to guide you through every difficulty.

Wise One, guide me through the maze of my circumstances. I am at a loss and I need your wisdom. Breathe your revelation light into my mind and let me see from your perspective. Oh, how I need you!

A Thankful Heart

I have not stopped giving thanks for you,
remembering you in my prayers.
EPHESIANS 1:16 NIV

In the light of God's presence, we find that what once went unnoticed is made clear. He has deposited his goodness in our lives; he has not overlooked anyone in his mercy. When we ask God to give us eyes to see where he is working in our lives, we can be sure that we will find him.

Gratefulness is a practice. As we stop comparing our lives with others and begin to cultivate thankfulness for what is already good in our lives, we will find our hearts attuned to the frequency of gratitude. Small joys are not insignificant. They add up to a glorious inheritance if we start counting. May we appreciate both the seemingly trivial and the significant blessings that fill our lives.

Good God, I want to see my life through your eyes. I have to believe that there is goodness to be found because you are present with me. Give me your perspective. Help me to look for your kindness in my life like I am searching for treasure. When I find it, I want to store it in my heart with the wrappings of gratitude.

Blessed to Trust

Blessed is the man who trusts in the LORD,
And whose hope is the LORD.
JEREMIAH 17:7 NKJV

Where there is confidence in our hearts, there is a cord of trust. If we are confident in ourselves, then we trust that we are enough. If we display belief in others, then we expect that they are capable of what we imagine of them. When it comes to the Lord, our confidence need never waver, for he is always shown to be faithful.

Where do our deepest hopes lie? Are they in our own abilities? Do they rely on others? Surely we will disappoint ourselves, and so will other people. We are not perfect but God is. He never wanders outside of mercy and kindness. His compassion does not shift or change. When our confidence lies in the Lord, we will find that it is never dissatisfied. May our hearts find hope in God, and may they never give up or let go.

Lord, you are the keeper of my heart. All my days are before you. You are not surprised by anything. I trust in your unfailing love to hold me close and guide me. My heart is bound to yours in hope. I know you will not disappoint me.

A Father's Help

The Spirit you received does not make you slaves, so that you live in fear again; rather, the Spirit you received brought about your adoption to sonship. And by him we cry, "Abba, Father." The Spirit himself testifies with our spirit that we are God's children.

ROMANS 8:15-16 NIV

As children of God, we rely on the help of our heavenly Father. We are not expected to provide for ourselves let alone fight those who would harm us. God is not just our help. He is protector, defender, provider, comforter, wisdom-giver, and constant companion. Why would we try to get by on our own when he is ready to offer us direction and aid?

We do not need to venture out of the safety of our Father's house only to fall prey to fear. We are part of a forever-family. We are not meant to get by on our own. We are not designed for isolation or self-preservation. Let today be the day we give up the fight of fierce independence. When we call out to our Abba, he always answers.

Abba, teach me what it means to be your child. Thank you that I do not need to rely on my own strength or knowledge to be successful in life. I have found the belonging I have always craved and was meant for within your arms. Keep me close, Lord, and lead me as I lean on you.

Working for the Lord

Just as you have always obeyed, not as in my presence only, but now much more in my absence, work out your salvation with fear and trembling; for it is God who is at work in you, both to will and to work for His good pleasure.

PHILIPPIANS 2:12-13 NASB

In relationship with our God, we find how to live. Jesus displayed that ministry was always meant to be fueled by connection with the Father. When we work, when we play, when we serve, and when we fellowship, we do it all as unto the Lord. There is no obligation we have that is outside of love.

Does this mean we are lazy in love? By no means! Love is the fuel that gives us the strength to do all that is before us. We need not struggle to find within ourselves the passion to keep working. It is God who fills us and revitalizes us so that we do what pleases him! He is the pure source of energy that flows through us to reveal his love through our lives.

Lord, partnership with you is an incredible mystery and wonder. You fill me with your love and mercy, and I get to give it away, constantly coming back to be filled again. The work I do is fueled by your grace. May I never go back to striving on my own.

God's Workmanship

We are God's handiwork,
created in Christ Jesus to do good works,
which God prepared in advance for us to do.
EPHESIANS 2:10 NIV

We were fashioned in the image of the Creator. It is in our design to reflect the beauty of God. There is no goodness displayed in our lives that is disconnected from him. When we see the resemblance of love, grace, patience, kindness, and mercy in our lives, we know that we are revealing our Maker.

We are not duplicates or cheap copies of some better model. God has created us each uniquely and wonderfully. We are not meant to be cookie-cutter. That was never the plan. But we were always meant for family. We belong to him. What we do, we do out of a reflection of our good Father. May our lives align with the fullness of our hearts which are overflowing with his compassion toward us.

Maker, you are so creative in your handiwork. You never duplicate your creation: not even two snowflakes or grains of sand are exactly the same. May I reflect your nature as I live out your incredible love. Fill me afresh today, Holy Spirit, with the fullness of your presence.

Rock of Refuge

My God is my rock. I can run to him for safety.
He is my shield and my saving strength,
my defender and my place of safety.
The Lord saves me from those who want to harm me.

2 Samuel 22:3 NCV

God is a safe place and shelter for those who call on him. He is the defender of the weak and liberator of the oppressed. When we have nowhere else to turn, we find that he has always been the firm foundation beneath our feet. We don't have to worry when we have God on our side!

When the storms of life rage and confusion covers our heads, where do we go for help? Our God is always at the ready; he's never late. May we trust the one who faithfully saves us time and again. His unchanging character stands the test of time.

Defender, you are the rock of refuge I run to today. Where I cannot see a way out of the trouble I am in, I trust that you will guide me. You are my safe place, and I take rest in you. Lord, come in power and rescue me.

God of Salvation

Don't hide yourself, Lord, when I come to find you.
You're the God of my salvation;
how can you reject your servant in anger?
You've been my only hope,
so don't forsake me now when I need you!
PSALM 27:9 TPT

God is near to the brokenhearted and close to all those who call on him. He does not leave us to drown in our circumstances. He is the God of our salvation; he will not forsake us! Even as we struggle in our desperation to find where God seems to be hiding, he will come through. He's already with us and he always has a plan.

When you find it hard to see where God is in the midst of your suffering, cry out to him. He is not far away. He will surely rescue you, and you will sing of his faithfulness again. Take heart!

God of my salvation, you have been my only hope—the thing I've been clinging to. Don't give up on me now! Come close and bring relief to the chaos that has me swirling. I cling to you as I wait for you. Let me see you today, Lord.

Present Joy

Surely you have granted him unending blessings
and made him glad with the joy of your presence.

PSALM 21:6 NIV

No matter what circumstances we face, the joy of God's presence is always available. His presence brings life, joy, and peace. It also brings comfort and healing. There is not a moment when he withdraws or withholds his nearness. He does not pull away to punish us; it is not in his nature.

May today be the day you find joy in the nearness of God. He always has an abundance of love to give. He is not a superficial giver; he will supply everything you need and often much more! Draw near to him even now; he is close.

My God, your presence brings life to my soul. I remember the joy I found in you in the early days of knowing you. Draw me to your heart again and revive my weary soul. Everything I long for is found in you. You are my hope and my home.

Slow Down

I wait for the LORD, my soul waits,
And in His word I do hope.
PSALM 130:5 NKJV

Slowing down and waiting with a peaceful heart is a practice. It does not come easy in this day and age where instant gratification is the expectation. When we consider the important things in life, however, rarely do any of them come with quick returns. Relationships take time and investment as do fruitful careers and ministries.

Patience and perseverance are not popular topics for spiritual growth though they are necessary. It is in the stillness where we find the rest we are looking for, and it is where we often find what we would otherwise miss in the go-go-go of our busy lives. With hope alive in our hearts, we may discover unexpected joy in the waiting.

Lord, as I practice waiting on you, I trust you to meet me with your goodness. Fill me with your peace and give me hope, teaching me to revel in moments of rest amidst the craziness of my normal life. You are worth waiting on. My soul finds restoration in you again and again!

Still Trusting

When I am afraid, I will trust you.
I praise God for his word.
I trust God, so I am not afraid.
What can human beings do to me?
PSALM 56:3-4 NCV

We cannot deny the reality of darkness in the world. There are wars and conflicts, atrocities and hatred being acted upon; there is brokenness and destruction to be found everywhere—from families to whole nations. And yet, God is light. He is truth. He is all-powerful. And he is present.

Where fear keeps you from seeing the bigger picture, dare to see from God's perspective. He has not left you, and he is not worried. Will you dare to trust him today? He holds everything together, and he has not forgotten a single promise that he has made. He will fulfill each one. He will not let you be overtaken, and he will not let you be crushed. He is better.

Good God, you are the hope of my heart and the lifter of my head. Calm the anxieties of my heart as I trust in you. May your loyal love fill me up and cause every fear to be overtaken. You are faithful, Lord, and I find that your grip on my life is sure even when I can barely hold on.

Saved by Wisdom

Wisdom and money can get you almost anything,
but only wisdom can save your life.
ECCLESIASTES 7:12 NLT

The Word of God reminds us of the power of wisdom especially throughout the Proverbs. Jesus' life is full of the wisdom of the kingdom. When he taught about the purpose of God's law, he reduced it to its simplest form—love. He instructed us to treat others in the same way we want to be treated. That, he said, is the essence of the teachings of Scripture.

This has not changed; it is still the standard. Do our lives align with this ageless wisdom? There is no higher law than the law of love. May we measure the success of our lives on this which is the foundation of everything else. May love be the thread that runs through our actions and our words. It is never too late to choose to walk in the way of love.

Loving God, you are the standard of all that is good, pure, and true. How could I but adore you when I consider your incredible affection? You are not swayed out of compassion or convinced to give up your relentless love. May my heart stay bound to yours in this same love.

Divine Power

His divine power has granted to us everything pertaining to life and godliness, through the true knowledge of Him who called us by His own glory and excellence.

2 PETER 1:3-4 NASB

The manifest presence of God is found within the person of the Holy Spirit who is our constant companion. We have fellowship with God, here and now, through communion with the Spirit. We have access to the power of God, alive within us, which gives us everything we need for life.

What is it that you need today? Do you need strength? Is it healing? Encouragement is found in him as well as perseverance and patience. There is so much more available than you could ever need. Where you have felt like you are running low, God has more than enough to fill you to overflowing. Let him meet your needs, the small and the large, with his powerful presence.

Holy One, I am so grateful that I am not left on my own to suffer through life as a beggar. I freely come to you as I am: you see me clearly. Fill me with everything I need today— most of all the power of your presence. Restore me to life again and breathe new hope in me.

Take Heart

*"I have said these things to you,
that in me you may have peace.
In the world you will have tribulation.
But take heart; I have overcome the world."*

JOHN 16:33 ESV

Jesus graciously revealed what it means to live a life of surrender to the Father while overcoming the world. Jesus taught us how to lay down our own rights in the name of love—even in the face of suffering. We cannot escape the troubles and sorrows that arise from our human experience, but we can experience God's grace and presence that leads us in peace.

May our hearts be full of courage as we live out the same love that Jesus did. He conquered the world, and we get to rest in his victory. We cannot add to what Jesus did, though we can live in agreement with it, refusing to strive for something that has already been accomplished. We have been brought from death to life and from darkness to light. We are no longer living as those in chains but in the freedom of Christ's victory.

Victorious One, I rest in your triumph. There is nothing outside of your power. I align my heart with yours today, taking courage and strength from the same power that raised Christ from the dead. Spirit, alive in me, I am your vessel. Fill me again!

Portion of Peace

"I am leaving you with a gift—peace of mind and heart.
And the peace I give is a gift the world cannot give.
So don't be troubled or afraid."
JOHN 14:27 NLT

God gives gifts that others cannot begin to dream of offering. The gifts are not contingent upon what we have to offer in return. We do not earn them based on our achievements. God's kingdom is not a rewards-based training program. What he offers he gives freely to all in the same measure which is always abundance! The peace of God, which goes beyond our understanding, is a gift straight from his heart to ours.

We cannot earn the peace of God. We do not need to strive for it, and we don't need to wait for a better day to receive what is always freely ours. Today, may we receive the peace of God in our minds, as well as our hearts—the peace that calms our fears and anxieties.

God of peace, you are consistently better than I imagine you to be. What an incredible reality that you give freely without asking anything in return. I offer you my mind and heart today, and I receive your peace that reaches to the depths of my soul.

Seeds of Goodness

Let us not become weary in doing good,
for at the proper time we will reap a harvest
if we do not give up.

GALATIANS 6:9 NIV

In life, there are seasons of sowing and seasons of reaping. There are times of creating and times of tending. There are moments of great joy and others of great sorrow. No matter where we find ourselves today, we can be sure that God is the same faithful Father in every season.

When we continue in the way of love, as we've been called to, we will not always feel content in it. It is a narrow path, sometimes rocky, continually requiring us to lay down our own rights for the sake of love. When we keep going, living as those who have been marked by God's incredible grace, we will be strengthened along the way. The coming fruit will be better than we can imagine.

Holy One, you see all my days clearly. When I am tempted to give up in my weariness, give me the strength to keep going. You are better than my best day, and more faithful than the rising sun. I give you today, which is all I have. Keep my gaze on you when my eyes begin to drift.

Never Without Hope

Those who love me, I will deliver;
I will protect those who know my name.
When they call to me, I will answer them;
I will be with them in trouble,
I will rescue them and honor them.

PSALM 91:14-15 NRSV

God is an ever-present help in times of trouble. He is the rescuer of the desperate, the defender of the weak, and a safe place for the wandering. He has never met a problem that he couldn't conquer, and there is no situation that is too much for him to handle.

Where in your life are you struggling to have hope? This is the very area where God can rush in and do what only he can do. He is your deliverer and your protector. He will rescue you and honor you. You may not be able to see how he will do it, but he will. He never fails.

Rescuer, I am so desperate for your help. Where I cannot fix my life, where I see no way out, I need you to come through for me. Fill me with your love and grace as I wait on you.

Good Gifts

Every good action and every perfect gift is from God.
These good gifts come down from the Creator of the sun, moon,
and stars, who does not change like their shifting shadows.

JAMES 1:17 NCV

The Creator of the universe—the Unchanging One—is the same one who is with us here and now in our present realities. He does not vary in temperament or intention. He is a good God who gives good gifts. When we consider the goodness in our lives, we can be sure that it is a reflection of the Father's love.

It is so easy to get caught up in the not-yets and the still-to-comes. When we look at our lives through the lens of lack, we can easily become overwhelmed by discouragement. When we start to recognize the things in our lives through the viewpoint of thanksgiving, our hearts will be changed by the encouragement we find. Let's take time to find the good in the details of our lives and be transformed by the renewing of our minds.

Unchanging God, you are the giver of good gifts. Give me eyes to see through your perfect perspective. When I look at my life, help me to see where you are already at work. I want my mind to be transformed by you. Fill me with your love, Lord.

Extravagant Mercy

Celebrate with praises the God and Father of our Lord Jesus Christ,
who has shown us his extravagant mercy. For his fountain of mercy
has given us a new life—we are reborn to experience a living, energetic
hope through the resurrection of Jesus Christ from the dead.

1 PETER 1:3 TPT

God has given us his own Spirit to empower us to live with hope beyond our understanding. Our minds can only do so much. Our hearts need to experience God's love and the breadth of his mercy as much as our minds need to understand. We are whole beings, and our whole beings need to know God.

His hope is living—it has an energy! May we experience the life of God within us in our bodies, spirits, and souls. His life inside of us is full of freedom. We can know this liberty that causes joy to erupt within us.

God of mercy, I want to know you with every part of me. Go beyond my mind and understanding; I want to know your love on a visceral level. Fill me up with your redemption life. I long to live in the freedom of your life within me.

United in Love

Be completely humble and gentle;
be patient, bearing with one another in love.
EPHESIANS 4:2 NIV

The fruit of lives partnered with Jesus looks like his nature toward us. Jesus, though the Son of God, was confidently humble. He knew who he was, and yet he did not make friendship with him difficult or exclusive. He was incredibly gentle with the weak and broken. He often took time to honor those who were overlooked and despised by society.

We know that we are reflecting Jesus' life within us when we choose love over everything else. In humility and kindness, not by force or arrogance, we reveal the heart of Jesus to those around us. When we keep choosing to love those who are difficult to even like, we are walking in the way of Christ. Let love be the fuel of everything we do.

Humble King, you are the pinnacle of mercy and kindness. Today I align my heart with yours, choosing to humble myself and consider that I do not know everything. Lord, you see how much I need you. Fill me today that I may pour out your love to others.

Slow to Anger

Whoever is slow to anger has great understanding,
but he who has a hasty temper exalts folly.
PROVERBS 14:29 ESV

In the vastness of God's love, there is patience, kindness, understanding, and mercy. He is not easily angered or set off. He is not on a short fuse. In the Father's heart, there is endless room for consideration and compassion. When we exhibit slowness to anger, we are revealing that our hearts are partnered with the Father's heart.

We have been shown incredible mercy by God, and not just once but countless times! In the same way, we live out what we experience. Let us choose to reflect the enormity of love we find in the Father as we learn to connect compassionately with others in our lives. May we be people of peace, grace, and understanding.

Father of kindness, you have shown your love in your compassion toward me. I cannot deny the power of your love that changes me. Fill me with your mercy that causes me to slow down and consider others before hastily reacting in my own interest. You are good, God, and I want to reflect your goodness in my life.

Faith with Patience

Be like those who through faith and patience
will receive what God has promised.
HEBREWS 6:12 NCV

Patience in practice is never quitting. It does not mean perfectly believing and hoping in every moment. It does not mean never doubting. It is facing the challenge of the present moments that threaten hope and pressing through even if just by sheer determination. Sometimes it looks like being discouraged one night and deciding to keep going the next morning.

God is faithful to fulfill his promises. That will always remain true. His timing, though, is often different than our expectations would dictate. In the face of waiting, do not give up hope. You will receive what you are promised. Keep believing even if it means wading through doubt on your way to the promise.

Faithful One, you do not change your mind based on shifting whims or desires. You remain constant in your intentions and loyal to your Word. I take hope in you as I press on. I believe that I will see your goodness in my life, Lord.

Alive in Christ

I have been crucified with Christ; and it is no longer I who live, but Christ lives in me; and the life which I now live in the flesh I live by faith in the Son of God, who loved me and gave Himself up for me.

GALATIANS 2:20 NASB

When we come to Christ and give him access to all of our lives, we find that he is the lifter of our burdens and the freedom-fighter of our souls. He has set us free from the chains of sin and death. We no longer live to serve ourselves and our own interests; we've been grafted into the kingdom of God where love's laws rule.

Where you are seeing the lack of love in your life, know that it is an area where God's presence can reach. It is an invitation to see the love of God, alive in you, fill you with the power of Christ's resurrection. There is nothing in your life that is outside of the realm of God's great compassion. Invite him into your weakness today and watch as he empowers you to live.

Son of God, thank you for paving the way to the Father's arms. You tore down every wall, and by your Spirit, you are alive within me. I will align myself with your kingdom today. Help my life reflect your goodness and character.

Tender Care

Warn those who are lazy.
Encourage those who are timid.
Take tender care of those who are weak.
Be patient with everyone.

1 THESSALONIANS 5:14 NLT

When we consider the fruit of the Spirit, it is all an expression of divine love. Joy, peace, patience that doesn't quit, kindness that is lived out, faith that withstands the trials of life: these are all proof of a life that is submitted to the Spirit. When you look at the fruit of your life, what do you find? Is it mostly self-focused, or does it point to the amazing love of God the Father?

When we practice encouragement, caring for the weak, and patience with everyone who comes across our path, we are living in the way of our God and King. The submitted lifestyle of a believer is one of overflow. We give away what we ourselves receive. Let us come to our God and receive the encouragement we need. Let us allow the Spirit to tend to us in our weakness. Let us keep coming to the Lord and find that his patience never runs out. From this place, we will live out what we experience.

God, you are good. You show me how to live in how you act toward me. Fill me up with your love that I may live out of the overflow of the abundance of your heart!

Never Disgraced

Those who go to him for help are happy,
and they are never disgraced.

PSALM 34:5 NCV

God is a help in times of trouble. He is the foundation that the faithful stand upon. He is the fulfillment of every longing heart. He is the same yesterday, today, and forever. He is always kind, forever merciful, and full of grace to all who come to him.

Today, take heart in the truth that those who go to God for help will never be shamed or dishonored. His heart is always full of compassion; he does not act in blind rage or annoyance. He is your good Father who always has words of wisdom to offer. What do you need help with today?

Holy Spirit, without fail, whenever I ask for your help, I have it. You know how weak I am; you are not surprised by my failures. I come to you and find an open heart every time. Give me the wisdom I need for the circumstances that are out of my depth. You are faithful!

Rest for the Weary

Take my yoke upon you and learn from me,
for I am gentle and humble in heart,
and you will find rest for your souls."

MATTHEW 11:29 NIV

Jesus is so patient with us. He is the embodiment of divine love. We find belonging and rest for our weary, searching souls in him. When we come to him, he lifts the weight of our heavy burdens. In the gentleness and humility of God's heart, we find that though we don't measure up by the world's standards, we are fully known and loved.

Will you come to him today with your burdens? He is not waiting to berate your choices; he will not shrug his shoulders in response to your problems. He has all the answers. Every solution you are looking for is found in his infinite wisdom. Learn from him and find the rest your soul desires.

Jesus, today I approach you with all that I have and all that I am. I trust that you will meet me with kindness and compassion. Lift my heavy burdens. May my heart find the rest I've been looking for in your presence today. Meet me and mark me with your love that changes me from the inside out.

August

I took my troubles to the LORD;
I cried out to him,
and he answered my prayer.

PSALM 120:1 NLT

Words of Life

I will never forget your commandments,
for by them you give me life.
PSALM 119:93 NLT

God's Word is full of instruction for our lives. More than that, we can clearly see God's character displayed throughout the ages. How merciful and kind he is. How full of love and compassion to all who turn to him. When we look for God, we will find him, for he is ever near.

As we turn our attention to the Lord, we cannot help but find that his words are full of life. Where we feel less-than and like we're not measuring up, the Lord lifts our heads and reveals that our worth is not at all dependent on our own goodness. He alone is perfect, and in him we are perfected. Where we have been striving, let us find rest for our souls. We don't need to try harder to be loved more; we can never be more loved than we are in this very moment.

God of truth, in you is life, hope, and joy. As I meditate on your Word, I find that my heart is strengthened and encouraged to keep walking in you. What a beautiful revelation is your unending love. Fill me afresh with the kindness of your heart today.

Wonderful Destiny

This is no empty hope, for God himself is the one who has prepared us for this wonderful destiny. And to confirm this promise, he has given us the Holy Spirit, like an engagement ring, as a guarantee.

2 CORINTHIANS 5:5 TPT

The Holy Spirit is our constant guide and companion. The Spirit freely gives us the wisdom we need whenever we need it. We have not been destined for destruction or destitution. Whatever we face in life, we do it with the strength and courage of our God who is with us, empowering us by his abundant grace. When we begin to despair, the Spirit draws near and covers us in the comforting embrace of his presence.

This is our promise and our hope—God with us! Until the end of this life, we are never left or abandoned; we are not expected to do anything in our own strength. May we lean into the love of our loyal God, who never wavers or changes his mind. What awaits us beyond this life is even better than anything we could experience on this earth. What a glorious hope!

Emmanuel, thank you for your constant presence in my life. When I start to fear for the future, remind me of your goodness and wonderful plans. May your presence be the strength I draw from in every circumstance. Every moment I am covered by your love. Fill me with your joy today.

The Victory Is His

The horse is made ready for the day of battle,
but the victory belongs to the Lord.
PROVERBS 21:31 ESV

There are no parts of our lives that lie outside of God's power. He is more than able at every turn and in every situation to do what we cannot. But does that mean we don't prepare ourselves? Of course we do. It is a necessary and privileged part of life to work to an end. Most of us do not have the luxury of devoting our lives to passion projects while neglecting the nitty-gritty of necessary, mundane work.

There is honor in hard work. As believers, we do not strive and toil for own worth, however. We do not work from a place of lack, but from the abundance of God's heart. And when we have done all that we can, we are yielded to God's ways that are higher. The victory is the Lord's. It belongs to him. When we have exhausted our resources, we are fueled by God's own storehouse of abundance. In fact, we have access to draw from this place at any point. What a relief!

Victorious One, thank you for your power at work in my life. Give me eyes to see your goodness on display in my life in little and large ways! Today, I draw from your strength. You are the source of everything I need. I rely on you, Lord—don't let me down!

Abiding in Freedom

*"If you abide in My word,
you are My disciples indeed.
And you shall know the truth,
and the truth shall make you free."*

JOHN 8:31-32 NKJV

God's Word is a light to our paths. It gives us a glimpse into the heart of our good Father, and it teaches us the way to live. Jesus' life and ministry is full of keys to living a life submitted to God. When we follow Jesus on his path of love, which is the harder way, we find life and freedom. It is so much better to follow him, where we are fueled by his compassion, than our own whims and desires which seek to gratify only ourselves.

Freedom is the ability to live unbound; we have the opportunity to choose what we do and where we'll go. We are unhindered by fear, lies, and self-imposed boundaries. The liberty that Jesus leads us into is full of opportunity, growth, and joy. Let us be connected to Jesus' life through the continual surrendering of our hearts to him. This is where we find everything our souls long for!

Jesus, your life brings me so much hope for my own. I am yours, Lord. My heart belongs to you. I want to follow in your steps of love. Your ways are better than mine, and I know that living for you will not disappoint me. Fill me with the light of the revelation of your love.

Reliable Trust

Those who know the Lord trust him,
because he will not leave those who come to him.

PSALM 9:10 NCV

The Lord of heaven and earth is constant and true. He is not reckless with his words, changing his mind from day to day. He is more reliable than the rising of the sun. His heart of love is purer than the clearest waters. He is not a man that he should lie, nor does he withdraw his compassion from those who call on him. He does not change his mind about us; his affection is unfailing.

When was the last time you considered the greatness of God's love toward you? How did it make you feel? Whether it is easy to trust or a constant battle of believing, you can be sure that the Lord is trustworthy and reliable. He will not leave you, and he will not fail you. His mercy is abundant, and it is yours today.

Lord, you are unfailing in love. I submit my heart, my mind, and my soul to you today. I yield my own intentions to you because I believe that you are better. You're better than my best intent; your love gives me the strength to live out of love. You are good, God!

Healing Wisdom

Do not be wise in your own eyes;
fear the LORD and turn away from evil.
It will be healing to your body
and refreshment to your bones.
PROVERBS 3:7-8 NASB

Our wisdom and knowledge is limited to our small understanding of a much greater, complex reality. When we submit our hearts to God in humility, we welcome his perspective that is much clearer than our own. When we open our minds to possibilities that lie outside of our own existence, we give ourselves the opportunity to grow in wisdom. When we listen and respect others, we also expose our hearts to insight outside our own realm of reality.

God is full of insight, freely giving his perspective to all who ask. When we look for it, we will find it. Because God's ways are higher than ours, and the way of love often costs us something even if just our pride, we find refreshing and healing as we follow his example.

Wise One, you never give stones when your children ask for bread. When I ask for your wisdom, help me to remember that the perspective I find in you is for my good. I submit my heart to yours, knowing that everything you do is fueled by mercy and kindness. You are not vengeful or tricky. You are reliable in love!

Forever Alive

The world and its desires pass away,
but whoever does the will of God lives forever.
1 John 2:17 niv

What an incredible hope we have in God. We do not live for this one, brief existence that passes too quickly. Though the world and its ways are momentary, our souls are not. We are eternal beings with the hope of an endless existence in the kingdom of our merciful God and King.

When troubles overtake us, where do we find our hope? Even if we face trial after trial, suffering after suffering, God's purposes and heart for us are not negated. He is full of mercy, compassion, and kindness to all. He does not change his mind. We can be sure that though the earth decays and nations fall apart, God is forever kind, and we belong to him. Let him be the hope of our hearts for as long as they beat.

God, you who are forever merciful, do not let my heart be overtaken by discouragement or despair. Give my heart the tenacity to hold onto your goodness no matter what is happening around me. You are better than my feeble mind gives you credit for. Don't stop moving, Lord. My hope is in you!

One Focus

I do not consider myself yet to have taken hold of it. But one thing I do:
Forgetting what is behind and straining toward what is ahead.
PHILIPPIANS 3:13 NIV

There is not much we can do about the past. Whether our upbringing was full of joy or trauma, our lives have been shaped by our history and choices. But that is not the end. What a relief it is that God is a redeemer. He is in the business of restoring broken things and making them new. As long as this day is called today, there is hope. He does not stop restoring us. He makes all things new; it's what he does.

As we are made new in his love, let us be encouraged to look at the goodness that lies ahead of us. It just keeps getting better. Even where there is suffering and pain, there is beauty to be found. We need not be discouraged by the past; when God comes in, he fills us with everything we could ever dream of needing. There is so much more to come. We have not reached our end. God is our hope and the fulfillment of every longing.

God, you are my one focus. I don't want to just get through my life; I want to live it with purpose, powered by your love that covers everything. Thank you for your covering of mercy. I can't help but be overcome with gratitude when I consider how you restore every broken thing.

Joy for Mourning

*Those who sow in tears
shall reap with shouts of joy.*
PSALM 126:5 ESV

There is no escaping the pain and grief that life eventually brings. When loss rips our hearts to shreds, it can be hard to imagine that we will ever experience joy again. It does not help us to pretend the pain away. Sorrow is as much a part of our experience on earth as pleasure.

We do ourselves a disservice when we expect that we should come to God only when we feel hopeful, confident, or happy. God is not surprised by our circumstances or at the agony that we experience. We discredit his love when we withhold our pain from him. He is the healer of the broken and strength for the weak. Let today be the day we come to God in our true states. He will not be disappointed, and as we let his love minister to us, we will find that we aren't either.

Restorer, you give joy for mourning. A dark night is never the end; the sun always rises. You are with me in the intensity of my pain. You do not ignore the suffering of my heart. You minister to me right where I am and bring me comfort. Come close today, Lord, as I draw near to you.

Comforting Compassion

Let your steadfast love become my comfort
according to your promise to your servant.
PSALM 119:76 NRSV

The compassion of Christ is a beautiful picture of the comfort we find in the presence of our kind God. He did not withhold mercy from those who were broken and wounded, but he healed them. He spent time with them, not requiring them to dress themselves up and come to the temple in order to find acceptance in his presence. Jesus, the humble king of heaven, met people where they were. Many, in turn, followed him.

How could we not fall in love with such a beautiful God? His requirement is the submission of our hearts, lived out in love not perfection. What a wonderful mystery! Where religion requires the keeping of laws in order to be holy, Jesus turned the system on its head. We find holiness in being united with Jesus in loving compliance. His holiness is our own, and we always find mercy and compassion when we need it.

Comforter, you are the one my soul finds rest in. When I fail, which is often, I find that you never change your mind about me. When my heart wavers, may your steadfast love strengthen me. You are the comfort I long for and the only one I need.

Until the End

"Teach them to obey everything that I have taught you,
and I will be with you always, even until the end of this age."
MATTHEW 28:20 NCV

God's ways are right and true. We can follow him knowing that he will lead us into his goodness even when we don't understand the conditions of our circumstances. When we love like Jesus, we embody God's character. We cannot go wrong if we live from that place.

As we follow the example of Jesus, we can guarantee that the path will not always be smooth. There will be times of pain. There will be hardships to endure. But we can be sure we are never alone. God is with us until the end of the age! There is not a moment or a day where he steps away. His presence is with us at every point. From him we receive everything we need.

Righteous God, you are perfect in leadership. You do not require what you did not give. As I follow you, Jesus, lead me in love. Strengthen me with the nearness of your presence even now.

Held Close

Even if my father and mother abandon me,
the Lord will hold me close.

PSALM 27:10 NLT

The strongest bonds we have on this earth pale in comparison to the strength of God's mighty love. He is more compassionate than the most loving mother. He is kinder than the most merciful father. He is a better friend than the most amiable brother. These relationships are but glimpses to a greater reality—a stronger love than we can imagine!

Even if our mothers and fathers disown us, the Lord holds us close with his loyal love. His affection never wanes even in the face of the depths of our humanity. He is infinitely better than we could ever give him credit for. When we feel isolated and we have no one to turn to, let us take hope in the closeness of our good God. He pulls us close and covers us in his powerful presence.

Faithful Father, you are better than anything I've known in my earthly relationships. Draw even closer and let me experience the goodness of your favor over me. I cling to you as you hold me.

Run to His Heart

It is impossible for God to lie for we know that his promise and his vow will never change! And now we have run into his heart to hide ourselves in his faithfulness. This is where we find his strength and comfort, for he empowers us to seize what has already been established ahead of time—an unshakeable hope.

HEBREWS 6:18 TPT

What an incredible hope we have in God. We run to his heart and find that we are surrounded by his faithfulness. He never backs out of a promise. When the storms of life threaten our peace and the trials of harsh circumstances wear down our confidence, God is the place of comfort and strength we run to.

We are empowered by God's grace to continue to trust and believe that all he says will come to pass. He has not given up and neither should we. But God is bigger than our belief. When we falter in faith, God is still faithful. If we do not give up, our hopes will not be disappointed. Today is an opportunity to be refreshed by his presence once again.

Loving God, you are the shelter from the storms of life. I depend on your presence to strengthen me in my weakness. Fill me with your love that pushes aside every fear. How they dim in the light of your goodness.

Light to See

The teaching of your word gives light,
so even the simple can understand.
PSALM 119:130 NLT

The truth of God's Word is not found in complex theories. The gospel is so simple and yet more powerful than the most intelligent mind on earth. In the light of revelation, we see things more clearly. As we meditate on God's Word, we find that the depth of God's character speaks to every part of our lives. There is nothing that is outside of his grasp. Nothing is hidden from him.

God's faithfulness covers everything. We can be confident in God's promises; they are always fulfilled. When we start to doubt, let us look into his Word and even to our own histories with him. We will surely see that he is a keeper of his word. He is with us at every turn. He is the light that brings clarity to every confusing situation. Let us continually look to him.

Yahweh, you are brighter than the sun. In you everything finds its rightful place. The chaos is returned to order in the light of your presence. Give me understanding where all I have is confusion. Light my path with your presence.

Not Disgraced

The LORD God helps me,
Therefore, I am not disgraced;
Therefore, I have set my face like flint,
And I know that I will not be ashamed.

ISAIAH 50:7 NASB

God is a constant help and friend. He lifts us out of the places we get stuck in and keeps us moving. With him as our defender and support, we won't be disgraced. He is more reliable than the most faithful friend we could ever have.

With God as your confidence, you can keep moving in the strength that he provides. Don't give up. But even if you do, he is with you constantly. He will not let you be ashamed as you work out your faith. Let your heart take courage as you rely on him to lead you through the maze of life. He sees everything clearly; you can trust his perspective. Take heart. He is your help and your companion.

Lord God, you are my shield and my portion. You are everything I need even when I don't know how to ask for it. Lead me on in your love and strengthen me as I walk with you. My confidence comes from your faithfulness. You are so good to me.

Generosity Returned

A generous person will prosper;
whoever refreshes others will be refreshed.

PROVERBS 11:25 NIV

When we look at God's character, he is anything but stingy. He is abundant in mercy, freely offering it to any who would ask. He has more than enough kindness to spare. He does not run out of compassion. He does not make us jump through hoops to receive forgiveness. He is always ready to pour out his love. He refreshes us constantly in his presence.

As God's children, we reflect his nature when we give in the same way. Are we sparing in our encouragement? Do we hold back love from those we fear will reject us? Do we withhold kindness from those we don't like? If any of these is true, today is the perfect day to change. As we extend the grace we have so willingly received, we are filled with even more. With God as our source, we will never run out of love to give.

Merciful Father, you are so full of goodness that you give away freely. Help me to live out of love, extending the same mercy I have received from your heart to others. Your way is so much better than my own. I align myself with you today, being filled up to pour out and then be filled again!

Daily Portion

Fill us with your love every morning.
Then we will sing and rejoice all our lives.

PSALM 90:14 NCV

God's portion is always measured out of his abundance. His love cannot be contained in boxes with tight lids. We are his vessels, filled by him and also poured out for him. We will never run dry with him as our source. When we are lacking, we simply need to ask, and we will find that we are satisfied once more.

With God's love filling us every morning, we have the strength and the sustenance we need to get through the day. We will go out rejoicing and return to be filled once more. Every moment is a new opportunity to be permeated by the compassion of God. May we never grow tired of it. How could we when it is life to us?

Loving God, you are so generous in mercy. I can't help but be thankful as you fill me up with your love again and again. Even when I grow weary of asking, you never hesitate to come through. You are abundant in kindness. Fill me this morning with a fresh revelation of your love.

Determined Steps

We can make our plans,
but the Lord determines our steps.

PROVERBS 16:9 NLT

God over all is God over each one. We make our plans and follow through on our action steps, yet God is the one who ultimately guides us. When our plans fall apart and our strategies are flawed, the love of God leads us on. We don't have to worry about how we will get through with God as our guide.

Though we may be discouraged when our ideas don't go the way we expect, this does not affect the faithfulness of God. We see in part and know in part, but God sees it all. He sees the big picture as well as every detail. What feels catastrophic to us is not a concern for him. May we find the peace we long for in the confidence of God's goodness toward us.

Lord, you are faithful in all your ways. I bind my heart to yours, trusting in your goodness even when I don't understand. I bring you my questions, but most of all, I offer you space to do what only you can do. Breathe peace into my heart and mind; I open my heart to you again today. Speak, Lord.

Test of Time

All flesh is like grass and all its glory like the flower of grass.
The grass withers, and the flower falls,
but the word of the Lord remains forever.
1 PETER 1:24-25 ESV

In a world where everything has an expiration date, it is hard to imagine anything that lasts forever. The Lord is eternal. He was before the beginning, and he will always be. When our hope is in him, it cannot be shaken for he is immovable.

In the light of what lasts and what does not, may we be people who invest in the eternal. Our flesh will die, just as the flowers fall and grass withers. But God will never fail. He does not decay. His Word is forever true. His faithfulness is without limit or end. May our hearts find confidence in the everlasting one who gives us new life. In him, we find undying hope.

Eternal One, your ways are right and true. I am so grateful that the suffering of this life is not forever. There is a much greater hope—life forever with you, unblemished and unmarred. My heart yearns for that reality even now. Lord, come with a taste of heaven's fullness. I open my heart to you today. Come and fill me with your unlimited love!

Faithful Protector

The Lord Yahweh is always faithful
to place you on a firm foundation
and guard you from the Evil One.
2 THESSALONIANS 3:3 TPT

There are so many unknowns in life. There are twists and turns; we cannot control our fate. Even when things seem to be going according to our expectations of life, we cannot predict every situation or outcome. When we let go of the control that has always been an illusion, we give ourselves the freedom to lean into the everlasting grace of our good Father.

God is faithful. He is the one who sets us in place. There are no mysteries to him. He is a reliable companion and a constant presence in our lives. He protects and guards us from the enemy who seeks to steal, kill, and destroy. God comes to bring life and not just a temporary fix. He is abundant in mercy, and he surrounds us with his comforting presence all the days of our lives.

Faithful One, I lean on you. Guide me and protect me as I follow you. I let go of the need to control my own outcomes. I trust your leadership because I know that you are good. Fill me up with your grace today!

Seen and Known

God will never forget the needy;
the hope of the afflicted will never perish.

PSALM 9:18 NIV

There is not one part of your life that is unseen by the Lord. Every need you have is clear to him. You don't have to worry whether God will come through for you; he always meets the needs of those who take refuge in him. Whether you see the way out of your situation or you're at a complete loss, put your hope in God. He is your ever-present help.

When you face problems that seem insurmountable, know that God has every solution. He will not fail you and he will not let you fall beyond his grasp. May today be the day your hope anchors deep in the love of God, empowering you to trust beyond your understanding. He is faithful to help you.

God, I take shelter in you today. You are where my help comes from. When I look around for answers, there are none to be found except in you. Be my rock of refuge. I hide myself in your goodness, knowing your presence will give me the life I long for.

Better Trust

The LORD is for me; he will help me.
I will look in triumph at those who hate me.
It is better to take refuge in the LORD
than to trust in people.

PSALM 118:7-8 NLT

When we look to the people around us for security and affirmation, it will only go so far. At some point, they will let us down. Even the most well-intentioned mothers, the purest-hearted friends, and the most loyal lovers will disappoint. The only perfect source is God himself. He is perfect in all his ways.

When the Lord is for us, who can stand against us? He is a help in times of trouble—right here and now! When we take our refuge in God, we are safe and secure. He will never let us down; it's not in his nature. When all seems lost and even those closest to us fail to meet our expectations, there is a better friend. The Lord will faithfully follow through on every plan he has made. Let us hope in him.

Lord, you are trustworthy and kind. As I look to you, fill me with courage to hope in your name and in your promises. You always come through. May my heart's confidence be in your faithfulness alone. You are so good!

Freedom for Captives

"The Spirit of the Lord is upon me,
and he has anointed me to be hope for the poor,
freedom for the brokenhearted, and new eyes for the blind,
and to preach to prisoners, 'You are set free!'
I have come to share the message of Jubilee,
for the time of God's great acceptance has begun."

LUKE 4:18-19 TPT

Jesus came to set the captives free. He led the way back to the open arms of the Father with his unmatched love that suffered the cross and the power that rose him up from the grave. There is no substitute for this kind of mercy. Where there are broken hearts, there is freedom. Where we are blind, he gives us new eyes. Where we are bound, he liberates us!

God's acceptance of us is unhindered and unmatched. The Spirit of the Lord—the same Spirit that was in Jesus—is alive in us today. There is no chain that can keep us from him, and there is no situation too hopeless that he will not turn it around. May the Spirit of God touch us with his power as we look to him.

Lord, you are the miracle maker. You free every captive with your strong love. Touch my life with your incredible power and redeem all that seems lost that is meant to be found in you.

Unseen Hope

In hope we have been saved,
but hope that is seen is not hope;
for who hopes for what he already sees.
ROMANS 8:24 NASB

In the chaos of what is right in front of our eyes, it can be hard to focus on what is unseen. God is near to the humble, and he binds up the brokenhearted in his life-giving presence. When we fumble in faith, still God is faithful. There is no challenge too great for him. He sees clearly and in clarity speaks from his unchanging goodness. He is full of love, full of hope, and full of joy.

When we lack in any of these, why would we try to stir them up in ourselves when we have access to the source of them? By leaning into his presence, we will find that we are filled with love, hope, and joy. Even when we don't understand how he could never tire of freely giving us his grace, we are benefitting from his generous heart. May we cling to the unseen hope we have as we press into him and ask for more.

Great God, you are the source of all life. Nothing thrives apart from you. Be my hope, my joy, and my strength as I walk through this life. Fill me afresh with your presence today that I may draw directly from your heart.

Powerful to Save

*Let us praise the Lord, the God of Israel,
because he has come to help his people
and has given them freedom.
He has given us a powerful Savior.*

LUKE 1:68-69 NCV

The God who led the Israelites out of captivity in Egypt is the same God who leads you into freedom today. Through Jesus you have been given access to the Father without condition. You are dressed in his mercy, and you cannot disappoint him because he sees you through the lens of perfect love.

Where you are experiencing defeat, know that the Lord is strong enough to save. He does not abandon his children to fear and torment; he will surely lead you on in his kindness. God is a help to all who are in trouble. Call on him today; he will lift you out of the ashes of the old and make you new again in him. He makes all things new including that which seems irreparable. Find your hope in him today; his power is at hand!

Powerful One, you are my Savior and my hope. When I tremble in fear and do not know where to turn or what to do, I cry out to you and you come to save me. It doesn't matter how many times I've needed your help; you are always quick in kindness and mercy. Thank you, Lord!

Taken Care Of

"People everywhere seem to worry about making a living, but your heavenly Father knows your every need and will take care of you."
LUKE 12:30 TPT

The God of the stars and the seas can provide for your every need. He is the best Father, taking care of his children with the abundance of his resources. Do you worry about where your food will come from? How about what clothes you'll wear? He will not let you go without sustenance or shelter. Don't hesitate to ask him for what you require!

Even in the midst of trials and suffering, God is nearer than you know. He does not abandon his children to the chaos of this world. Where you struggle to see his provision, may you have revelation to see where he is already at work. Where there is tremendous need, God is the God of miracles, and he will not let you down.

Good Shepherd, you are reliable in love and you always provide for every need I have. Draw near today in your presence, that I may know the comfort of your nearness and the warmth of your love. I need you more than anything, Lord. Encourage me in your presence.

Keep Going

I have fought the good fight,
I have finished the race,
I have kept the faith.
2 TIMOTHY 4:7 NCV

There is no defeat in this life that is final; though failures are inevitable, the mercy of God is even more predictable. Perseverance is a virtue of following God, not because he is cruel but because this crazy world is. What does it take to keep going? When we have exhausted our own resources, we turn to God who is abundant in everything we could ever need. In fact, what if we were to live from that place in the first place? His life in ours is our strength and our joy!

Whether you find yourself in a season of struggle or one of ease, be filled with the strength of God as your fuel for living. When you don't know what else to do, lean into the heart of your Father that never changes. He is always abundantly compassionate and merciful, offering you the power you need to persist. He will get you through any and every scenario—just watch him do it.

Holy Spirit, you are my help and my strength. I depend on your support in this life. When I struggle to even want to go on, come near and empower me with your presence. I am yours, Lord!

Mercy Cries Out

O Lord; give ear to my pleas for mercy!
In your faithfulness answer me, in your righteousness!
PSALM 143:1 ESV

The Lord is near to the humble and to the brokenhearted. His mercy is never far away. It is closer than you know. When you fear tomorrow, the peace you experience today is affected. Do not hold back from the Lord. Make this an opportunity to find that his nearness is the very courage and strength you need.

When you are overcome by the unexpected turns of life, it may be hard to find your grounding. Do not hesitate to cry out to God; he never disengages! His ear is always tuned to your voice, and nothing goes unnoticed. Whether with a shout or a whisper, he hears you. Even the unspoken cries of your heart are noted. Do not despair in the midst of the unknown. Lean into your good God who is closer than the skin on your bones.

Merciful One, I won't stop calling out to you. You're my only hope! Where fear is threatening my peace, breathe your perfect love into my heart that stills the chaos. I am calmed in your presence. Come and be my portion today.

Tenderhearted

Be kind to each other, tenderhearted,
forgiving one another,
just as God through Christ has forgiven you.
EPHESIANS 4:32 NLT

In this harsh world, it takes practice to remain soft. Where our hearts are prone to harden in defense, God has offered a different way. When we represent the life of Jesus in our own lives, it is not done with harsh speeches or cold distance. Jesus was always approachable, ever near to the humble and the outcasts. He didn't turn away hearts that willingly sought him out.

What then should we do? How should we live? As those who are quickly offended? May we be as forgiving to others as God has been to us. Let us stay tenderhearted in relationship, offering kindness and mercy where we are tempted to bruise with our words. As we have been shown incredible compassion, may we freely give away sympathy with hearts that are in tune with our Father. And where we lack the desire to do it, may we draw from God's endless supply.

Loving God, you are better than any person I have ever known. Fill me with your heart of love that offers mercy freely. I want to look like you in love. I offer you myself again. May your love overflow from my life.

Radiant Truth

The precepts of the LORD are right,
giving joy to the heart.
The commands of the LORD are radiant,
giving light to the eyes.

PSALM 19:8 NIV

The teachings of God are full of wisdom for life. They are not rigid rules to follow like soldiers falling in line in their regiment. The principles of God are in perfect alignment with his wonderful nature. He who is full of lovingkindness and mercy gives to all in the same measure. He is generous in compassion and never lacking in power to save.

When we consider God's Word, do we think about a list of regulations, or do we see an invitation to relationship? God is not a taskmaster who issues orders like a general. He has given us keys to abundant life in him through the life and ministry of Jesus. Though we cannot avoid pain in this world, we certainly can benefit from the abundant grace found in partnering with God in this life.

Gracious God, your ways are wise and your heart is true. You don't fluctuate in consistency. Why would I question your ways when you are constantly faithful and good? I align myself with you and your kingdom today. Empower me to follow after you and live like you.

Strong Joy

Don't be sad,
because the joy of the LORD
will make you strong.
NEHEMIAH 8:10 NCV

There is not a moment of our pain that goes unnoticed by the Lord. When we are overcome by sadness, we are not left to wallow in it. He comes with the power of his presence when we look to him. He covers us in love, awakening our hearts to the wonders of his goodness. When we have nothing to offer, there he is pouring out his compassion that strengthens us.

What a marvelous mystery—the joy of the Lord fills us with the strength we need to keep going. And what is the joy of the Lord? Are we not his joy? He has abundant delight in us and in restored relationship with him. We are continually filled with his powerful presence that never leaves us. The pleasure of God's heart is the power of our lives. What wonderful news!

Father, it is such a mystery to me that you are full of delight over me. I can't comprehend that kind of love, but I want to! Flood me with revelation to understand your affection in a new way today. There I will find my strength!

September

All of God's promises

have been fulfilled in Christ

with a resounding "Yes!"

2 CORINTHIANS 1:20 NLT

Live Above Anxiety

"I repeat it: Don't let worry enter your life.
Live above the anxious cares about your personal needs."
LUKE 12:29 TPT

Life is found in the yielding of our hearts to the one who holds us together. We do not need to strive to get everything on our to-do lists done to be successful. When anxieties and worries flood our senses, how do we ground ourselves? May we be people who lay down our lives in submission to love.

God is faithful to show up, faithful to provide. He will do what we cannot. Press into his heart of love today. Let that be the fuel for your motivation. Do what you can and leave the rest in God's hands. He is trustworthy and dependable. His love will never let you go or let you down.

Faithful One, I submit my worries and my cares to you again today. I know that you are more powerful than any doubt, question, or denial. Fill my heart with your hope that brings me life. As I trust you, lead me in your peace.

Citizens of Heaven

We are citizens of heaven, where the Lord Jesus Christ lives.
And we are eagerly waiting for him to return as our Savior.
PHILIPPIANS 3:20 NLT

This world is not our ultimate home. We are not bound to a broken system and society forever. We are subjects of the kingdom of God, and his ways supersede the laws of this world. When we begin to despair at the brokenness we face in this realm of reality, may our hearts be encouraged by the superior law of love in which heaven operates.

There is no height or depth that can separate us from the love of God in Christ Jesus. We are made fully alive in him even now in the waiting. May our courage be strengthened to live in the example of Jesus, knowing that his return is surely coming. He will not disappoint, and his timing is perfect.

Jesus, you are the hope of the nations and the expectation of every longing heart. I belong to your kingdom which is eternal. Fill my heart with your love today and teach me to walk in your ways of wisdom. May I be aligned in mercy and kindness, reflecting your compassion in my life.

Wonderful Plans

Lord, you are my God;
I will exalt you and praise your name,
for in perfect faithfulness you have done wonderful things,
things planned long ago.

ISAIAH 25:1 NIV

God's ways are higher than our ways and his thoughts are above our own. He is fully aware of every possibility and choice before us, and he is not worried for our future. He is full of wisdom for all who ask, and his plans faithfully work out time and again.

God is not stingy, and he does not withhold from anyone who seeks to understand his ways. How could we not praise him for his faithfulness when we look and see all that he has done? And he is not finished. He works in wonders and miraculously saves his people. We are firmly planted in his perfect love that will not disappoint because we are his.

Lord my God, I belong to you. Give me eyes to see your goodness where I have only seen my lack. Fill my heart with the revelation of your love at work within me, right here and now. You are better than my most vivid imaginings. Be glorified in my life and work out your wonderful plans!

Promise of Life

That faith and that knowledge come from the hope for life forever,
which God promised to us before time began.
TITUS 1:2 NCV

When we face trials and doubts, loss and great sorrow, it can be difficult to see past the dark void of closed doors. We cannot wish death or destruction away; in this life, we must walk through the valley of pain where all of our doubts creep out of the corners of our minds. But this is not our downfall. This is not the end.

Our hope lies in the promise of life forever without confusion, pain, or destruction darkening our days. God has promised us a beautiful eternity of fullness of life in him. We come to Jesus, the way to the Father, and he welcomes us into his heart and his home forever without blame or harsh requirements. In this short span on earth, we get glimpses of this glory, but our present reality will pale in comparison to the magnificent actuality of the kingdom to come!

Keeper of my days, you are the life inside of me. You give me a glimpse of the glory awaiting me on the other side of eternity. I am full of hope! Give me flawless faith to cling to you, no matter what I may face in this short life. You are all I have to hope in.

Confessed and Forgiven

If we confess our sins, He is faithful and righteous to forgive us our sins and to cleanse us from all unrighteousness.

1 JOHN 1:9 NASB

God is merciful and kind; he is quick to forgive, like the patient and compassionate Father he is. When we confess our hearts to him—even the pieces we try to keep hidden—he accepts us and covers us in mercy. None of us is righteous on our own, but God covers us in his righteousness, marking us as his children. It is the generosity of our Father to wrap us in his character.

What have you been keeping from the Lord? There is no shame, no hidden flaw, no poor choice or series of them that can keep God's love from pouring over you. It is always more than enough. There is nothing outside of his reach or his compassion. Bring him the wounded, tarnished parts of your heart and watch as he cleans them up and restores them. He is more loving than you can imagine.

Father, I come to you with all that I am today. I don't want to hold anything back from you. Make me new in your love, covering every part of me and flushing fear out of my system. I invite you into my whole being. Wash me in your compassion and mercy. Refresh me in your living waters!

Born Again

All praise to God, the Father of our Lord Jesus Christ.
It is by his great mercy that we have been born again,
because God raised Jesus Christ from the dead.
Now we live with great expectation.

1 PETER 1:3 NLT

We have been born into the family of God through resurrection power. The same power that raised Christ from the dead is the power accessible to us through the Holy Spirit. We have God alive in us and with us in every circumstance. When we consider that mysterious and glorious reality, how could we bow to fear?

God could have called us servants—made to do his bidding. And yet, he has always been about family and companionship. We are not slaves to fear; our God is the King of love, abounding in compassionate mercy. Our expectations are based on his goodness not on our experience. We are sure to see his goodness alive in our lives because we belong to him.

God, you are abundant in power that saves. Fill my mind with the awareness of your goodness at work in my life. I know that you are present; I know that you are with me. Give me eyes to see through the lens of your perspective that my heart may hope in you alone.

Led to Repentance

Or do you despise the riches of His goodness, forbearance, and longsuffering, not knowing that the goodness of God leads you to repentance?

ROMANS 2:4 NKJV

When we look at the world's leaders, there is not much goodness and kindness to be found. Though we may find one, still viewpoints are biased and actions limited. God, however, is full of lovingkindness toward all. He does not favor the rich or promote the powerful. He gives the same portion to all—his abundance. He is close to the weak, strengthening them. He is near to the humble who have no other options.

How could we despise the goodness of our God toward those who call on him? Who are we to judge? We are all led to the heart of a kind, welcoming Father with the same mercy he extends to everyone who approaches him. We are not punished by love; we are drawn in by it. May we be full of the same patient love and kindness as our good Father.

Kind God, you are the one who draws me to yourself in love. I find the freedom I didn't know I needed in your presence, where you make me come alive in your affection. I turn away from lesser things and offer you my whole heart again.

Detail Oriented

*"Don't worry. For your Father cares deeply
about even the smallest detail of your life."*
MATTHEW 10:30-31 TPT

God is a master of details, not missing a single element. God is over everything. He is not too big to be concerned with the details of our lives. He sees it all, and not only that, his Word says that he cares deeply. We so often get caught up in the particulars of our lives while losing sight of the bigger picture. God does not have that problem.

He sees both the big aspects and the small completely clearly. So, then, we need not worry. He is involved in the intricacies of our lives all the while leading us into the plans and purposes of his heart for us. May we boldly walk arm-in-arm with him, trusting his leadership without apprehension. He is dependable and honest, always leading in love.

Holy One, you are wise in all your ways. I trust you with my life, knowing that you know better than I do. I harness my heart to yours; fill me with the confidence of your love and sprinkle my life with your goodness. My hope is in you, Faithful One.

Clothed in Dignity

Strength and dignity are her clothing,
and she laughs at the time to come.
PROVERBS 31:25 ESV

There is confidence that rises in us when we know who we are and what our lives are aligned with. Belonging to the kingdom of heaven, we are clothed with strength and dignity. We have honor because the King of heaven has given it to us. We can know that no matter what may come, our worth never changes. It cannot be altered by shifting circumstances.

May we be full of confident joy as we move throughout our days. Knowing that our value is not contingent upon our output or the conditions of our lives, we can walk with the poise of dearly loved children. We are covered by goodness in every moment.

Wonderful God, you have covered me with your love and said that I am your own. What a glorious mystery! I am grateful to be found in your arms, my good Father, covered by your very nature. May I live with the confidence of heaven fueling my hope. You are so good.

Good Advice

Wise people can also listen and learn;
even they can find good advice in these words.

PROVERBS 1:5 NCV

In the wisdom of God's heart lies every key to every question we could imagine asking. He is full of good advice and guidance for all who seek him. There is no mystery too great that cannot be solved by leaning into the Lord. Though it is not an instant search for knowledge, the journey we take on wisdom's way will lead us along God's path of goodness.

When we look in God's Word for instruction, we will find it. Even more, when we get to really know God's nature through his faithful Word and presence with us, we discover that the fruit often reveals the source. When we don't have explicit direction for where we should go or what we should do, we can be confident that God goes with us, and we will know he is at work when we see the fruit of his love in our lives.

God of wisdom, I hunger for your truth today. Fill me with your love that leads me to life. When I am not sure about the decisions I will make, give me confidence in your nature alive within me. Help me to trust that your Spirit will guide me, no matter what. I want to walk in your way, Lord.

Worship Him

Come, let us bow down in worship,
let us kneel before the LORD our Maker.

PSALM 95:6 NIV

When we offer God the reverence and devotion he deserves, we align our hearts with his good character. He is worthy of our adoration. The maker of heaven and earth is the same one who fashioned us each with our unique traits that reflect aspects of his image.

Let us come to God with our whole hearts laid open before him. Let us give him the honor that he is due. He is faithful and will always be. He is full of lovingkindness to all who seek him. He is better than we give him credit for; we only see in part, but he is wholly divine and glorious. May today be the day where we set aside our list of cares and simply love him because he is worth being adored.

Holy One, you are worthy of all my praise and devotion. You deserve all of my trust; I won't hold it back from you today. Be glorified, Lord. Your love is better than life!

Led by Mercy

You in Your mercy have led forth the people whom You have redeemed;
You have guided them in Your strength to Your holy habitation.

EXODUS 15:13 NKJV

God is redeemer of the broken and rescuer of the weak. He is liberator of the captives and protector of the vulnerable. He leads us in kindness, never requiring more than we have to give. He is patient in love, always giving compassion to everyone who looks to him.

God is not weak in kindness. Rather, we find that there is incredible strength in mercy. God is powerful to save, and save he does! May we never be disappointed in God's merciful heart that extends forgiveness to all. Instead, as we are lovingly led by the presence of God, may we find that there is power in kindness. Power to unite instead of tear down. Power to heal rather than injure. May we walk in our Father's footsteps.

Merciful God, thank you for leading in kindness. I want to be just like you! I will not hesitate to follow your path of love that leads to life. Teach me to walk in your way. I know that it is better than my own.

Followed by Goodness

Surely goodness and mercy shall follow me
all the days of my life,
and I shall dwell in the house of the Lord forever.
PSALM 23:6 ESV

God's character is marked by his goodness. When we look at our lives and see through the lens of his mercy, we find that there is evidence of him all around. If we cannot see it, we only need a shift in perspective. His Word is a lamp to our feet and a light to our path. Where we follow him, even when we cannot clearly see, there is evidence of his life.

There is not a day where we are without God's presence. He is with us in the here and now, in every moment of our lives. We cannot escape his Spirit. When we turn our attention to him in the present moment, we train our eyes to look for him and our ears to listen for his voice. He has not left us to our own devices. If we look, surely we will see the goodness and mercy that are already here.

Present Lord, you are the one my soul longs for. When I question whether I can go on, I am reminded that you are with me. Where you are, there also is your love that permeates everything. Open my eyes to see where your goodness has been in my life. Your mercy is surely with me.

Keep Me Safe

Do not, O LORD, withhold your mercy from me;
let your steadfast love and your faithfulness
keep me safe forever.

PSALM 40:11 NRSV

We are kept secure within the safety of God's unwavering love. His faithfulness is our shield when we face uncertainties. He does not deny us kindness when we look to him. He is full of unfailing love that holds us up through the storms of life.

When we are desperate, it's hard not to let anxiety and worry overtake our minds. Our nervous systems respond to the stressors naturally. But God is our Maker. He knows the intricacies of our minds and bodies. As we look to him, we will find the peace we long for. Let us fix our minds on the steadfast love of the Lord that doesn't change with the seasons. He is the same yesterday, today, and forever.

Lord, you are one I cling to in the storms of life; I depend on you to carry me through when I cannot put one foot in front of the other. In my weakness, I rely on your strength. And when I feel strong, you are still the one who holds me. Thank you for your constant presence, faithful God.

Miracles of Mercy

Lift your hands and give thanks to God
for his marvelous kindness and for his
miracles of mercy for those he loves!
PSALM 107:8 TPT

When God shows up in power in our lives, our grateful hearts can't help but praise him for his goodness. He does not fail in his love, and he never will. In the waiting, may we remember his faithfulness that marks everything he does! It is not foolish to hope in the Lord, for he will prove to be trustworthy.

When we see God's provision and answers to prayer in the lives of those around us, we can celebrate with as much gratitude as if it were our own fulfillment. Watching him show up for others will encourage our hearts on our own journeys if we let it. God's faithfulness to one is his faithfulness to all. Take heart today; celebrate with those who celebrate and pray in believing with those who are waiting.

Kind God, you don't stop working in miracles of mercy. You haven't changed the way you operate, and you certainly haven't given up. When I struggle to believe, may my heart be encouraged by what you are already doing for others as well as in my own life. Open my eyes to see your goodness where it currently is.

Carried by Love

In all their affliction He was afflicted,
And the angel of His presence saved them;
In His love and in His mercy He redeemed them,
And He lifted them and carried them all the days of old.

Isaiah 63:9 NASB

God has never been distant. Even before Jesus arrived on the scene, God was full of tender care and love for his people. The one who was faithful is the one who remains faithful to his Word. He does not leave us alone in our suffering and re-enter our lives when we're in a better place. He is constantly with us, carrying us when we cannot continue on our own.

What a relief that God's manifest presence is always available to us. We are never left alone, and he does not expect us to drag ourselves through this life. We were always meant for connection, and we were always meant to eat from his table of plenty. We are not beggars seeking crumbs and leftovers but sons and daughters that have unhindered access to a bountiful feast.

God, you have been my portion all my days. I have tasted of your goodness. Carry me in your merciful love when I do not have strength. I come to your table of abundance and eat my fill. You are so, so good!

Chosen by Compassion

"I will have mercy on whom I have mercy,
and I will have compassion on whom I have compassion."
ROMANS 9:15 NRSV

God is unendingly compassionate. His mercy has no beginning and no end. We cannot convince God to withdraw his mercy from anyone—even ourselves! He is more loyal than the most devoted lover. His tender care is deeper than the affection of the most loving parent. He really is that good.

Have you disqualified yourself from being known as his own? It does not matter how many times you fail; as long as you humbly return to him, you are welcomed in. Once marked by his love, you will always bear his signature. There is no need to run from him when you mess up. Turn around and run right into his arms instead.

Wonderful God, you are so much better than I give you credit for. When I am tempted to withdraw from you, lure me in again by your love. As I turn my heart toward you, I remember your amazing love that covers all my shame. Love me to life again!

Honored by Goodness

The LORD God is like a sun and shield;
the LORD gives us kindness and honor.
He does not hold back anything good
from those whose lives are innocent.

PSALM 84:11 NCV

When we were brought into God's family, adopted as his children, we were once and for all covered by his mercy that cleansed us from all unrighteousness. Hidden in Christ, our lives are innocent. We do not need to worry about whether we qualify for God's goodness. He is the one who qualified us in the first place.

God brings honor to us even in our deepest shame. When we allow him to minister to the dark places of our hearts, his light shines and all that was hidden is made clear. He mends the wounds and binds up the brokenness. God is in the business of making things new, and he will do it for us. He doesn't just do it once; he continually heals, restores, and saves. He doesn't grow weary of loving us to life.

Lord, you are abundant in love and plentiful in mercy. What an amazing mystery that you don't get tired of pouring out your love. My heart takes hope in that truth today. Here I am, Lord. Fill me again.

Peace to All

The Messiah has come to preach this sweet message of peace to you,
the ones who were distant, and to those who are near.

EPHESIANS 2:17 TPT

The love of God is all-inclusive. There is no one left out of the kindness of his heart or the mercy that he extends. He came as a peace-bringer for all who would listen. And that is what he is. He gives us the confident assurance of hope in the quiet knowing of our hearts. Where there is chaos, there is an invitation for his peace to enter in.

Are there areas of your life that feel out of control? Let the perfect love of God fill your mind, heart, and body as you submit yourself to him. Where you can do nothing, it is an opportunity for God to do something better than you could even imagine. God's peace is less like a quiet library and more like a sweet, joy-filled adventure with a loved one. It is unhindered communion, and it is yours through Christ.

Lord, your peace is so much better than the ups and downs of most of my relationships. You don't ever change, and you never argue your case with me. You are patient, kind, and true, and I want to be just like you. May I be a harbinger of peace in my sphere of influence.

glory to god

Not unto us, O LORD, not unto us,
But to Your name give glory,
Because of Your mercy,
Because of Your truth.

PSALM 115:1 NKJV

God's character is unflawed. There are no hidden faults in his nature or places of deception within his heart. He is faithful to his unending mercy and lovingkindness. When we consider his greatness, we may find that our problems feel smaller. In the light of his goodness, we may discover that our flaws are no match for his relentless love.

When our hearts are surrendered to the King of kings, his nature will show up in our lives. We will see his goodness, mercy, and truth, not because of how great we are but because of his greatness. He eclipses our feeble attempts to love with the expanse of his tender love. What good news this is for us! We don't rely on ourselves but on him. To God be the glory, for it is only through him that his mercy and truth meet any of us.

God, all glory be to your name. There truly is no one else like you. You are selfless in love, generous in kindness, and never lacking in mercy. What a wonderful reality!

Storms Stilled

He awoke and rebuked the wind and said to the sea, "Peace! Be still!"
And the wind ceased, and there was a great calm.
MARK 4:39 ESV

When the storms of life rage, it can take everything within us to not panic and fear the worst. When we consider that the one who calmed the seas is the same one living within us, we have no need to fear being overtaken by storms. The same power that split the sea so that the Israelites could escape Egypt is the same power available to us.

God is not a one-time help in times of trouble. He is an ever-present help in trials and storms. The one who was once with us is the God who is with us now. May our hearts take courage in his faithfulness; may they take rest in his power at work within us.

Jesus, you once spoke to the waters to be still, and the raging storm calmed. I need you to do the same in my life. Speak to the tempest in my soul to be at peace, and my heart will find rest. Where my life is out of control, bring order like only you can. I rely on you!

Fully Supplied

I know what it is to be in need, and I know what it is to have plenty.
I have learned the secret of being content in any and every situation,
whether well fed or hungry, whether living in plenty or in want.
I can do all this through him who gives me strength.

PHILIPPIANS 4:12-13 NIV

Whatever circumstances we face today, we can be sure that God has supplied us with everything we need. God is our provider and our sustainer. Where we cannot see how we will cope or get through, God offers us his unending grace that empowers us to life.

Don't lose heart today. Keep pressing on and pressing into him. He never leaves you on your own. When you can't see a way out of the trouble you face, God is with you right in the middle of it. Just as he was in the fiery furnace with Shadrach, Meshach, and Abednego, so he will be with you. Take hope in your ever-present King today; he is the source of strength and power.

Holy One, you are the hope of my heart. As my heart trembles at the thought of all this life requires, I remember that you are the strength that keeps me going. I cannot do it on my own. Draw nearer still, Lord!

Truth Persists

The very essence of your words is truth;
all your just regulations will stand forever.
PSALM 119:160 NLT

The wisdom of God is pure and well intentioned. Our kind and merciful God does not seek to control us with blind rule following. His teachings and principles are full of his compassion. He directs and guides us through his Word. He leads us in loyal love.

When we follow God and seek his truth, we won't be disappointed. His thoughts are purer than our own, and his ways are full of wisdom. When we submit our lives to him in humility and trust his intentions, we will find that he always knows better than we do. We may think our ways are good, but when we fail, we see that the discernment of God is a guide for our own good! May we trust his truth as we follow him.

God, you are so much better than I am. My intentions are faulty, but yours are always pure and peace-loving. May my heart find strength to follow your lead even when it initially resists. Your ways are so much better!

Covenant Covering

I know that you will welcome me into your house,
for I am covered by your covenant of mercy and love.
So I come to your sanctuary with deepest awe
to bow in worship and adore you.

PSALM 5:7 TPT

It is a wonderful gift that we have been welcomed into the house of the Creator of all life! We don't come by our own merit; we don't earn entrance by our good deeds. It is God's covenant of mercy that covers us. He has done everything necessary to welcome us into his presence, and we need only come to him.

We can't help but be transformed by the goodness of God that covers us. His incredible love wraps around us like a blanket, comforting us and bringing us rest. What a wonder that the belonging we are looking for has nothing to do with what we offer. We simply enter into this relationship and reap all of the benefits. As we are changed, so will we reflect this same kind of mercy and goodness to others.

Lord, thank you for your covering that allows me to enter your presence. I can't help but adore you when you are indescribably good. Fill me with your mercy that I may embody it in my life. I'm so thankful for your incredible love that changes everything.

Cling to God

You shall fear the Lord your God;
you shall serve Him and cling to Him,
and you shall swear by His name.

DEUTERONOMY 10:20 NASB

When we walk in the way of the Lord, which is the path of love, his goodness and mercy are all over our lives. We cannot follow him and be left out of the covering of his love. It's just not possible. Sometimes it is hard to see what is around us in the dark. As we cling to God, allowing him to lead us through the black of night, we cannot clearly understand what, if anything, is growing. When the day breaks and the sun rises, we will see that his goodness has been there all along even when we could not comprehend it.

Don't lose hope if you are in a dark night. On the other side, you will see the evidence of God's mercy with you every step of the way. He is trustworthy. Just hold on and keep going.

Father, I rely on you to come through for me again and again. I cannot escape your goodness even if I try! When your light shines on my life, I see the treasures that were hidden in darkness all along. You are my strength, Lord. I depend on you.

Turn to Me

Answer me, O LORD, for your steadfast love is good;
according to your abundant mercy, turn to me.

PSALM 69:16 NRSV

There is no end to the mercy of God. His steadfast love has no interruption, and there is nothing we can do to talk him out of his compassion. When our hearts need to remember his goodness, do we not recount his faithfulness? He has been constant through the ages, consistent in kindness.

Where do you need a touch from the Lord today? What does your heart need? May the remembrance of his goodness to others and in your own life stir up hope again. He is more than able, more than willing, to meet you right where you are today. You don't have to clean yourself up or dress up your unbelief. Just come and ask. According to his unfailing love and overflowing mercy, he will meet you.

Holy One, you are the one I come to in the hour of my need and in the time of my rejoicing. You see my heart, just as it is right now in this moment. Meet me with your love, Lord. I can't pretend that I don't desperately need it. Here I am: meet with me.

Blessed to Receive

*"Blessed are the merciful,
for they shall receive mercy."*
MATTHEW 5:7 NASB

One of the principles of the kingdom of God is that with the same measure we use, it will be shown to us. If we refuse to show mercy to others, mercy will be withheld from us. If we do not forgive others, how can we receive forgiveness? If we do not make room for more by giving what we have away, then there is no space to receive. God is bigger, even than these principles, but why would we want to withhold something that has been so freely given to us?

In love, we choose to love others. May our hearts be filled up as we pour out. God will not leave us dry, and he does not expect us to budget our love. His heart is always full to overflowing. Why would we operate as those who have a limited supply when our source is the Source of all life? Let us live generously, for in generosity we will receive!

Merciful God, you are full of lovingkindness. Even as you pour out more, you never diminish in compassion. You are my supply! Fill me up that I may pour out, and I will return for more. You are so generous, Lord.

Kind God

The Lord is righteous in everything he does;
he is filled with kindness.
PSALM 145:17 NLT

In all things, God is good. He is better than the most reliable, kind-hearted, forgiving person we could ever know. He never wavers in consistent love. The more we get to know him in relationship, the more we find that he is better than we could have ever imagined.

We can trust God's ways because we know his amazing nature. The things that hold us back from him are limited; they don't complete the whole picture. When we surrender our own understanding and see from God's perspective, we align with him in trust. His love is pure and we can depend on it all the days of our lives.

God, you are kind in all of your ways. Your patience reflects this—even just your patience with me! I believe that you are better than I have even tasted. I surrender to your ways, Lord. Fill my life with your wisdom, peace, and truth.

Love's Image

*"Love your enemies, do good to them, and lend to them without
expecting to get anything back. Then your reward will be great,
and you will be children of the Most High, because he is kind to the
ungrateful and wicked."*

LUKE 6:35 NIV

The mercy of God is always freely given with no conditions.
When we live with the same kind of generosity, we will find that we
are reflecting our Savior. The path of love is not the easier way to live
because it constantly calls our ego into submission. When we lay
down our own rights, we will find the life that the Spirit imparts to us
is so much better than the pride we could find in our own success!

When you consider what it would look like to live a life of
kindness, not expecting immediate return for your investment,
how does that make you feel? There is a reward awaiting those who
live humbly loving others without agenda, and it is straight from
God's hand. Dare to let your heart consider what love's image looks
like in your life.

*Most High, you are the way, the truth, and the life. Your
ways are so much better than my own; I won't run away from
your love, and I won't hold back from your heart. Strengthen
and empower me to follow after you no matter what.*

Heard

The Lord does not listen to the wicked,
but he hears the prayers of those who do right.

PROVERBS 15:29 NCV

If you are reading this, there is an openness in your heart to consider that God can change your life. To be right with God, you simply submit your heart to him and ask him to cover you in his love. He will wash away every blemish and every stain that keeps you from seeing his goodness. The wicked are full of pride and think they know everything, but the humble admit that there are things outside of the realm of their understanding.

We approach the throne of grace with boldness, knowing that God hears us. And if he hears us, surely he will answer us. He is faithful in love and mercy, always extending kindness. We don't need to fear that he will ignore us, or worse, turn us away. It is not in his nature to deny compassion to a seeking heart. He is always reaching out in love—always!

Lord, I have no goodness on my own, but in you I see redemption and life all around me. I depend on you to transform the broken, chaotic parts of my life. I know that restoration is yours alone. God, come and make all things new in my life.

October

Jesus Christ is the same yesterday
and today and forever.

HEBREWS 13:8 NASB

Living Expression

The Living Expression became a man and lived among us! And we gazed upon the splendor of his glory, the glory of the One and Only who came from the Father overflowing with tender mercy and truth!

JOHN 1:14 TPT

Jesus was and is the full expression of God. He who was God from the beginning confined himself to flesh and bones so we could know the fullness of his love lived out in human form. When we lack wisdom in life, we can look to the example of Jesus. He wasn't just a model for relationship with the Father, he is the fulfillment of every hope we have. He was, he is, and he will always be.

Jesus' story didn't end at the cross or the grave. In his resurrection, he was raised to life forever, and he once and for all defeated the curse of death over us. We are raised to life in him, first by fellowship with him, and secondly when this life is over and he redeems everything. What a hope and what a foundation! May our hearts find encouragement in the legacy of Jesus here and now, which is always available to us.

Merciful God, you are full of tenderness toward me. Your truth supersedes my logic and understanding. Fill me with the revelation of your wisdom. I want to walk in your ways, truly knowing your heart. Help me where I fail to understand and give me tenacity to trust in every circumstance.

Peace with God

*Since we have been justified by faith,
we have peace with God
through our Lord Jesus Christ.*

ROMANS 5:1 ESV

When you have a bad day, how does that affect how you view your relationships? Do you find yourself uncomfortable with yourself or others, or do you take comfort in those closest to you? God never changes his mind about you. If you have submitted your life to Jesus, then you are at peace with him, and not even the worst day full of your poorest choices can change that.

Thank God that we do not rely on our own perfection to find peace in him. He freely gives mercy to us, and we can never deplete his resources. Where troubles have us on edge, may the reality of God's goodness in making us his own calm our anxieties.

Good God, thank you for being the one who does all the heavy lifting in this relationship. I am perfected in you, covered by unfailing love. Refresh me again in your presence where my heart is brought alive in you. I need you more than the air I breathe.

Kingdom of God

The kingdom of God is not eating and drinking,
but righteousness and peace and joy in the Holy Spirit.
ROMANS 14:17 NASB

When we are overly concerned by the needs in our lives, it can be difficult to feel at peace. Thankfully, God has an endless supply within his kingdom available to us through his presence. The Holy Spirit is the conduit of never-ending grace, peace, and joy.

What are you lacking today? Do you need more hope? How about joy? God will not leave you dry as you call on him. He is so much more than a provider though he certainly never leaves us without what we need. His Spirit is always with us, freely filling us with the goodness of his kingdom. Do not hesitate to invite him to meet you today with the abundance of his love. As he draws near, you won't be disappointed.

God, your kingdom is so much better than the courts of the most lavish kingdoms on earth. Though rulers feast on the finest foods, I have access to something even better—the fullness of joy, peace, and love through your Spirit at every moment! Fill me again today, Lord.

Watched Over

*The LORD keeps you from all harm
and watches over your life.
The LORD keeps watch over you as you come and go,
both now and forever.*

PSALM 121:7-8 NLT

Fear is a strong force that either keeps us stuck, propels us into hasty decisions, or causes us to run away. Perfect love is full of clarity, wisdom, and the freedom of choice. It is unhurried and peaceful. There is power in the stillness it provides to the chaos. The Lord is rich in love, not wishing for anyone to waste away in torment. Where fear has been a motivator, may God's rich mercy overtake it.

The Lord sees your every step. He does not turn away as you move through this life; he doesn't miss a moment. He is the keeper of all of your days. What is the driving force of your life today? Is the confusion of fear running the show, or is God's love and wisdom your guide? You will know the difference in the fruit of your heart and life. Where there is peace, there is God. Press into that today.

Lord, you are the keeper of my life. I know that you see me and you walk with me. You keep me from harm as I walk in the way of love, choosing your wisdom over my own. Where fear has overtaken aspects of my life, I ask for your perfect love and peace to replace it. I receive your kindness over every area.

Looking Up

To you I lift up my eyes,
O you who are enthroned in the heavens!
PSALM 123:1 NRSV

The pace of life is incredibly hurried. There is always more to do, and since we are often connected digitally, there is pressure to perform in unreasonable ways at an extreme pace. There are countless demands on our attention even recreationally. We need never take the time to pause and reflect, or to set down our phones in order to observe the world around us. However, this is not how we were meant to function. We need fresh air and other people. We need time and space to rest without the nagging of potential projects always in the back of our minds.

When was the last time you took more than a few minutes to step away from the demands of your life and just rest? Did you take a walk or play with kids or animals? Similarly, when did you last look up to the heavens just to gain perspective? Whether cloud-watching by day or gazing at the stars, when you direct your gaze up, you may be surprised at the shift in perspective it brings.

God, you are enthroned in the heavens, yet even they can't contain you! You are so much bigger than my little life, but you are still concerned with me. My heart is relieved when I think about how much greater than me you are; I find hope in your power and higher perspective.

Satisfied in Him

They shall neither hunger nor thirst,
Neither heat nor sun shall strike them;
For He who has mercy on them will lead them,
Even by the springs of water He will guide them.

Isaiah 49:10 NKJV

God is perfect in mercy and abundant in power to save. He guides us with his wise leadership. He provides for every need. We will not go hungry or thirsty. He protects us from the harsh elements, and he leads us on paths of peace in his presence.

Does this seem too good to be true? Even so, it is the way of love. If it doesn't sound better than we dare hope, it is less than the promise of fellowship with him. We cannot bypass pain in this life; yet, even as we walk through suffering, God is our provider. He is a shelter. His mercy never fails; it is always more than enough for everything we face. We walk in the communion of relationship with the Creator as our guide. What a wonderful gift!

Merciful God, my soul finds everything it needs in you. I am satisfied by your persistent presence that fills me with goodness beyond my imaginings. Lead me in your perfect wisdom, Lord. I am yours!

Answer Me

O Lord; give ear to my pleas for mercy!
In your faithfulness answer me, in your righteousness!
PSALM 143:1 ESV

When we grow weary in our circumstances, reliving the same cycles over and over, it can be difficult to keep asking God for healing and redemption. When we find it hard to hope, will we abandon faith or will we keep pressing into him even when we can't see the way out?

God is always faithful. He doesn't change his character based on the length of our troubles or the attitudes we have concerning them. He is so much better than that. His love is constant in every circumstance. Where we struggle to see the light of his goodness in our lives, may we never stop crying out for his help. He is always nearer than we know.

Lord, you are my saving grace and the help I rely on. There is no one like you. Do you see my desperation? I can't hold back my cries for your mercy to show up again in my life. I depend on your faithfulness like I need water to survive!

Renewed

He saved us, not on the basis of deeds which we have done in righteousness, but according to His mercy, by the washing of regeneration and renewing by the Holy Spirit.

TITUS 3:5 NASB

God's ways are without equal in this world. He is full of compassion for all, never turning away a hungry heart. He will not let the helpless be overrun by evil. Salvation is through him alone. We don't need to dress ourselves up or be high achievers to earn the mercy of the Lord. It is a free gift to all, provided straight from his presence.

The Holy Spirit cleanses and renews us with the kindness of God. It's not anything we've done—it's all him! What an amazing reality that he covers us in pure love. May we be filled with the power of his presence that awakens our hearts to life. He ministers to the wounds of our souls, reaching the depths of us. He heals our broken hearts. May his wonder-working Spirit continually change us from the inside out.

Holy Spirit, you breathe life into me and awaken parts of my soul that I thought were gone forever. You restore the innocence of my inner child and give me eyes to see my past through your faithfulness. You are so good. Don't ever stop doing your wonderful work in my life.

Springs of Life

How priceless is your unfailing love, O God!
People take refuge in the shadow of your wings.
They feast on the abundance of your house;
you give them drink from your river of delights.
For with you is the fountain of life;
in your light we see light.

PSALM 36:7-9 NIV

God is a refuge for the weak, abundant provision for the needy, and full of delight for those who drink from his presence. When we look to him, we find that things in life become clearer. Questions are answered and solutions reveal themselves. In God's love, we will never find ourselves lacking any good thing.

Do you feel overrun by the troubles of life? Run into his love today. His presence will never fail to both guard and strengthen you. Drink from the river of his delights. If sadness is what you bring to him today, do not be discouraged. He will wrap his presence around you with comfort and feed your soul with the sweetness of his heart.

Unfailing One, you are the one I cling to. I come to you with all my lack, every need, and the raw reality of my emotions today. I know they are not too much for you. Surround me in your presence and satisfy my heart with the kindness of yours.

Dazed with Despair

*My inner being is in depression
and my heart is heavy, dazed with despair.*
PSALM 143:4 TPT

Depression is not a new phenomenon. The worries of this world have always been heavy. The burden of suffering is an age-old experience. When sadness follows us like a gray cloud, it can feel as if the sun will never shine again. But our feelings do not predict God's faithfulness. What good news that is! The light will shine on us again; it will burn away the fog of despair.

When our hearts are heavy, let us find comfort in the arms of our good God. The Spirit is our comforter, and he is nearer than the breath in our lungs. He will not let us go—not ever! He is the lifter of our burdens, and he shares his strength with us whenever we need it. Even today he is close.

Holy One, surround me with the comfort of your presence, and come nearer than you've ever been. May I taste the goodness of your heart today—I know that it is sweet. Override the worries that swirl around my mind with your perfect peace. You are the lifter of my burdens

Victory

Every child of God defeats this evil world,
and we achieve this victory through our faith.

1 JOHN 5:4 NLT

Our lives are hidden in Christ. Every failure and every success is covered by him. We need not despair our disappointments when God is where our ultimate triumph is found. He has equipped us with everything we need to live an abundant kingdom life through his Spirit. He always gives in generosity and not begrudgingly.

There is an easy way to predict whether you will live a life of purpose or not. If you are a child of God, you belong to his family and you inherit the fruit of his kingdom. You will not be overcome with evil, but you will overcome evil with good. That is the promise of God in your life. Find your strength in him today. He will not leave you without.

God, as your child, I rely on your power to strengthen me to live with your goodness pouring out of my life. Even when I cannot see it, I know that you are working within me because I am yours! You are my victory, and you never, ever fail.

Kindness Matters

Kind people do themselves a favor,
but cruel people bring trouble on themselves.
PROVERBS 11:17 NCV

In a power-driven world, kindness is often brushed off as weakness. The ways of this world are marked by ease and efficiency, while the ways of the kingdom are marked by mercy and peace. The world is about tasks and the kingdom is about relationships. This is not to say that nothing gets done when we follow God, but the importance is always on relationship. People always come before work.

This can be seen in the golden rule, which Jesus said summed up the whole law. We should love God and love others as we do ourselves. When worth is an inherent value in humanity rather than a reflection of what a person has to offer, kindness is a natural reaction. May we be full of compassion in our interactions with others.

Compassionate One, you are full of kindness to all. As your child, I want to reflect that same mercy in my own life. Where I am prone to overlook others in favor of my own agenda, gently remind me of the most worthwhile endeavor—to love.

Grace Given

"I will make all my goodness pass before you and will proclaim before you my name 'The Lord.' And I will be gracious to whom I will be gracious, and will show mercy on whom I will show mercy."

EXODUS 33:19 ESV

When we look for God, we will surely find him. He does not stay hidden when we are searching for his goodness. He is endlessly compassionate. He cannot be talked out of his mercy. He is incredibly kind in his dealings with us, and he often gives us much more than we ask for.

Do we trust God's wisdom in our lives? He does not require obedience for his own sake. He does not need a bunch of people falling in line, blindly following his regulations. What he wants—what he has always wanted—is companionship. What a wonder that we can know him in the beauty of his goodness. His wisdom is for our good, and that is always the case. May we trust his ways because we trust his heart.

Gracious God, you are beautiful in your mercy. Thank you for freedom to know you. As I draw near, you come closer still. Lead me in the power of your present love today.

Faithful God

Know that the LORD your God, He is God, the faithful God who keeps covenant and mercy for a thousand generations with those who love Him and keep His commandments.

DEUTERONOMY 7:9 NKJV

How often do we realize that we'd completely forgotten about a memory when someone else mentions it? With this in mind, how often do we spend in remembrance of important things in our lives? There are so many things that slip our consciousness; it is utterly human for this to happen. As we practice recollection, we may be surprised at the beauty we rediscover.

God's faithfulness is a marker of his character; it never changes, and he never fails to keep his covenant. As we look through our histories with the lens of his loyalty, our hearts will inevitably fill with gratitude. He who has done it before will do it again. He won't ever stop.

Faithful One, give me eyes to see where you have been working in the story of my life up until now. I want to see from your perspective. Spirit, open my heart to yours as I look for you. I know that you hear me. You are so faithful.

Abundant Peace

*May mercy, peace, and love
be yours in abundance.*
JUDE 1:2 NRSV

In a world where we fight scarcity on multiple levels—emotionally, physically, and mentally—a God who freely gives in quantities of abundance can be a foreign concept. God doesn't give us just enough to survive in the moment, he gives more than we need in most cases!

Where we are longing for peace, God grants it freely. Where we need mercy to meet us, there it is in plenty. Where our dry souls long for love, there is a river of compassion flowing toward us. As we receive from the generous heart of our good God, we can't help but begin to act with the same approach to others. We won't become whole versions of ourselves by accident; we are filled to overflowing with the goodness of the Holy Spirit who transforms us.

Good God, you are my portion of mercy, love, and peace. The measures you use are not the same as the world's, and for that I am beyond thankful! There is always more than enough to both receive and to give away. Your love is full; it is rich and satisfying.

Wholeness in Him

May the God who gives us his peace and wholeness be with you all.
Yes, Lord, so let it be!
ROMANS 15:33 TPT

In a world of competition and never enough, we may be dissatisfied with what is good in our lives, always looking to what could be better. The problem with this is that we miss what is already wonderful. How will we ever be satisfied later if nothing is good enough in the here and now?

God is present in this very moment. His peace is ours right now. If the fullness of his presence is ours, then we have everything that is good available to us right here. He is wholly accessible in this moment, and in him we are made whole. Why do we wait to obtain something later when it is ours for the taking now? May we press into him today and find every longing satisfied in his presence.

God, you are the one who brings healing and wholeness. I don't want to waste another moment waiting for the right time, when the right time is now. You are good, you are here, and you are mine. Come and fill me, Lord. Not with a portion, but with the fullness of your presence.

Dependent on God

It depends not on human will or exertion,
but on God, who has mercy.
ROMANS 9:16 ESV

When was the last time you got off the merry-go-round of life to rest for a time? The pace of this life will not let up; if you are waiting for a better time to take a day off or a less busy season to start that hobby you've been thinking about for months, that time won't ever come. Perhaps it's time to reconsider what priorities look like.

Thankfully, the value of our lives is not dependent on our own output or intentions. God has already declared that we are enough in him. Why are we so easily convinced that meaning is wrapped up in what we do? Much more accurately, it is who we are. God's mercy covers us in our weakness and in our strength. May we lean into his heart, taking our cues for living from his wisdom and not from the expectations of the world.

God, I find my true value in you. As I look to you, I can see myself more clearly. Thank you for your wisdom that is always available. I want to live like you, not according to the expectations of my perfectionist views or of anyone else's beliefs about who I should be. I lean on you, God!

Close to Him

The LORD is near to all who call on him,
yes, to all who call on him in truth.

PSALM 145:18 NLT

When we feel isolated and alone, the depths of the pain can intensify. In our sadness, even calling a friend can feel like too much—if there's one that will answer us to begin with. But God is always there when we need him. He is closer than a brother; he is always at the ready to come to our rescue when we call on him.

Like a close, trusted friend, he can read between the lines. There is no need to pretend with him; we couldn't hide the true state of our hearts from him even if we tried. There is no distance too great that he would not cover it. He closes the gap between what we feel and the reality of his presence with the ease of his ready comfort. Let us call to him in our dismay. He won't hesitate for a moment.

Lord, your nearness is my strength. You hold me up with the comfort of your presence. I need you today, God. Come and blow through the caverns of my soul. Bring light to the darkness within me and heal my wounds with the salve of your love. I am yours!

Accompanied by Love

Be strong and courageous.
Do not be afraid or terrified because of them,
for the LORD your God goes with you;
he will never leave you nor forsake you.

DEUTERONOMY 31:6 NIV

When fear keeps us from moving forward, what can we do? Do we succumb and talk ourselves out of whatever it was that lay on the other side of that fear? Do we try to find another option around it? God's Word is full of statements that encourage us to take courage. We are not meant to buck up and not be afraid because of what we are capable of. Our strength lies in who goes with us!

We are not alone in our challenges, and we are not left to figure things out on our own. Where worry tries to convince us that we are not enough to keep going, faith says that although we can't work things out by ourselves, the one who is with us every step of the way is able. The all-knowing, all-powerful, merciful one is our constant companion and confidant. We cannot lose when we are accompanied by him.

Lord, you are the champion of my heart. You have clear vision and endless wisdom, and I lean on you. When fear threatens my resolve, come closer and speak your words of life. Give me perspective to see your wonderful goodness with me every step of the way.

Goodness and Mercy

Oh, give thanks to the LORD, for He is good!
For His mercy endures forever.

1 CHRONICLES 16:34 NKJV

When we look at the state of our lives and can only see what's lacking, it is disheartening. The anxiety that rises with the unknowns of circumstances and the pain that we can't seem to escape can feel like too much. If what God says is true, he is always good and his mercy goes on forever, so there must be some hope hidden within the lining of our lives.

God is always with you. He never leaves. He does not take days off and he doesn't move onto greener pastures. Wherever you are today emotionally, physically, and mentally, he is with you. It is not too much for him to handle. He is not stumped by how to help you. He knows exactly what you need. He is good. His mercy is yours and you will see the fruit of his nearness in your life.

Merciful God, give me eyes to see where you are moving in my life right now. I yield my heart to you. I don't want to wallow in self-pity. I want—I need—to know your wisdom. Thank you for never leaving me. Come closer even now.

God of Justice

The LORD waits to be gracious to you,
and therefore he exalts himself to show mercy to you.
For the LORD is a God of justice;
blessed are all those who wait for him.

ISAIAH 30:18 ESV

In the waiting, hope can feel like barely grasping a flimsy wish—like holding the string to a helium balloon that at any moment could float out of our grasp, never to be recovered. In reality, hope is more like roots going down into the soil; we cannot see how far they go, but they soak up the nutrients and cause growth above the ground. Hope that is rooted in the soil of God's love cannot be lost.

God is not fickle; he is stable in mercy and steady in compassion. His justice is better than any we've ever seen exemplified on this earth. His pure motives qualify him to judge in an unbiased way. As we trust him, we will not be disappointed. Nothing goes wasted in his kingdom. We will find, in the end, that he pulled everything off perfectly.

Just One, you stand alone in wisdom and in love. Keep my heart entwined with yours that I wouldn't give up hope in your unfailing mercy. Keep me in the safety of your presence and fill me with your goodness. Give me the strength to keep walking with you.

Generations of Mercy

*His mercy is for those who fear him
from generation to generation.*

LUKE 1:50 NRSV

Whether we are first-generation believers or we come from a long line of lovers of God, the fruit of families following him is full of mercy. As children of God, we reap the benefits of those who have gone before us. God is as faithful today as he was yesterday. He is as devoted in this present age as he was in the days of Abraham, Moses, and David. His character has not changed one iota.

If you are a new believer, don't hesitate to learn from those who have walked with God for longer. Get in community; as you share life with other lovers of God, you will find that their faith will build your own. If you have been living your life for God for a significant amount of time, reflect on God's goodness in your life and in the lives of those around you. How has his mercy shaped you?

Faithful God, you never stop leaning in close with mercy. My life is yours. As I share my life with others who are going after you, I am encouraged by your faithfulness. You never stop loving, redeeming, and comforting. Thank you.

Great Kindness

LORD, answer me because your love is so good.
Because of your great kindness, turn to me.

PSALM 69:16 NCV

God's response to us is never based on our own goodness. He does not require perfect examples of holiness in order to help us. Thank goodness! The Lord answers us out of the kindness of his own heart. We are met by love at every turn. He will never meet us with anger, disappointment, or dismissal.

Consider the parable of the prodigal son. When Jesus shared this story with his disciples, he was clearly revealing the way the Father deals with us. After the son had gone away from his father's house, squandered his inheritance, and lived out his rebellion, he was left with no options but to come back and beg for a place as a servant in his father's house. And what was the father's response? As soon as he spotted his son approaching, he ran out to meet him, wrapped him in his own robe, restored his identity, and threw a huge celebration. This is the same love that meets us every time we come to God.

Kind Father, who else is like you in your tender mercy? I know that whenever I approach you, you come quickly, never hesitating in love. You are so good to me!

God's People

*Once you were not a people, but now you are God's people;
once you had not received mercy, but now you have received mercy.*
1 PETER 2:10 ESV

When we consider our lives hidden in Christ, what is the fruit? We have been welcomed into a loving family where we are fully accepted as we are. The mercy that covers us has imprinted us with the seal of God's approval. We belong to him. He will never shut us out or take away our rights as his children.

Have you felt vulnerable in your place as God's child? Do you feel like at any moment you could lose your position? Take heart today; you have been adopted into God's inclusive family. No one else could ever take your place, and you can't lose your spot at his table of plenty. What is yours now is yours forever. You belong to God, and he belongs to you.

Good Father, I am so grateful to be your child. Encourage my heart today in your love; remind me what it means to be your own. I won't be tricked into believing that I don't belong anymore. You have said that I do, and your word is the only one that matters!

Compassion Overflowing

*"Show mercy and compassion for others,
just as your heavenly Father overflows
with mercy and compassion for all."*

LUKE 6:36 TPT

As we are met with love when we spend time in the presence of God, we are filled to overflowing. What a wonderful relationship we have with our kind God. Just as we are shown mercy and compassion over and over again, may we show the same kindness and forgiveness to others.

When we love others without condition or expecting any benefit in return, we are reflecting the love of the Father that freely gives to all without asking for anything. Even in this giving, we have been filled by the power of God. Nothing that we give away was ours to begin with. We are met with the kindness and compassion of God every time we approach him. Every day is a new opportunity to be filled up and poured out, ad infinitum!

Merciful Father, everything that you require is found in what you freely offer. I cannot help but sing of your goodness when I consider that you don't put conditions on your love. May I love in the same way, constantly being filled up to flow out to others.

To Be Known

I will be glad and rejoice in Your mercy,
For You have considered my trouble;
You have known my soul in adversities.

PSALM 31:7 NKJV

There is nothing within our lives that is hidden from the sight of God. He sees every detail: every question in our hearts, every courageous act of faith, and the underlying beliefs that fuel our actions. He sees our victories and he sees our defeats. More than that, he comes to our aid time and again, never leaving our side.

When life takes a drastic turn and the foundations that we thought were permanent begin to crumble, God is near. What can be shaken will be, but his faithfulness, love, and mercy will not be removed from your life. Just as God knows you in every season of your soul, you will also see and know him in every high and low. When you look back over your life, the thread of his faithfulness will be clear to you.

Constant One, your presence is life to me in every season. Be near, Lord, even today. I need your perspective, wisdom, and grace.

My Savior

Guide me in your truth and teach me,
for you are God my Savior,
and my hope is in you all day long.

PSALM 25:5 NIV

When we don't know where to turn in the chaos of life, there is a sure place of comfort and safety waiting for us. When we take a break from trying to find solutions to the problems we face, we will find rest in the arms of our Father. The presence of God is near and it is powerful.

You don't have to do any more today to earn your place at the feast of your God and King. Why don't you lay down your burdens and find rest in him today? He will guide you in truth and teach you, but you don't have to lay the groundwork right now. If you are overwhelmed, now is the perfect time to take a moment to direct your attention to God and let him breathe life into you. He will transmit his peace even now.

Savior, you are my help all day long. When I stop and take a moment (or ten) to direct my gaze to you, I find that you meet me with love every time. You alone are my hope, God. No one else is like you.

Treasured Truth

Your laws are my treasure;
they are my heart's delight.
PSALM 119:111 NLT

The laws of the Lord are full of his characteristic kindness and mercy. He does not demand anything that he does not give us the resources to live out. He leads us in his unmatched wisdom on the pathway of life. He does not guide us into destruction; everything he does is to build us into pillars of his love. He restores the wasted years and rebuilds the ruins that the storms of life left in their wake.

His faithfulness is unparalleled. Our hearts will fill with delight as we watch him work everything out for our good! Where there is pain, he comes with healing. Where there is shame, he brings mercy that completely disarms it. As we follow in God's ways, we find that his nature is visible everywhere we look. He is so worthy of our trust.

Good God, I follow you as you lead me on the path of your pure love. Even in the trials, I know that your goodness will prevail. You will lead me into life: of that, I'm sure. My heart is yours, Lord. Continue to guide me.

Medicine for the Soul

A joyful, cheerful heart brings healing to both body and soul.
But the one whose heart is crushed
struggles with sickness and depression.
PROVERBS 17:22 TPT

God's nearness brings us joy unspeakable. Even in the valleys of deep despair, with God by our side, he is sowing peace into the paths we tread. When our hearts are broken, he comes in close as the comforter. We don't need to worry about the sadness that weighs us down. God meets us right in the middle of it and holds us. He carries us when we have no strength to move on our own.

The joy of the Lord is fortified within us in the constant connection we have in his presence. We are never disconnected from his heart. The relief we find in his nearness is a balm to our souls. He refuels our waning reserves of love. He meets us with the power of his compassion in every season. May we find the restoration our souls long for in the nearness of the source of all life.

Holy One, your presence is full of joy. Heal my heart as you fill me with the power of your presence. I rely on you today and every day.

Met by Compassion

Blessed be the Lord!
For he has heard the voice of my pleas for mercy.

PSALM 28:6 ESV

When we don't know where to turn in our distress, and our hearts feel completely sapped of all strength and hope, let us turn to the one who knows us better than we know ourselves. Every time we call on him, he hears us. He meets us with mercy every single time. There are no exceptions to his lavish love.

You cannot weary God with your requests. Don't rely on yourself to figure a way out of your mess—there's no need to! Lean into the love of your Father as you call on him. He will rush to meet you and give you the wisdom you so desperately need. He will not fail you. The impossible is possible to him. Let him handle this for you.

Compassionate One, you are full of mercy every time I call out to you. I weary of my own requests, but I am reminded today that you never get tired of my voice. I won't hold anything back from you. I find relief in your presence.

Completely Covered

Amazingly, God—so full of compassion—still forgave them.
He covered over their sins with his love,
refusing to destroy them all.
Over and over he held back his anger,
restraining wrath to show them mercy.

PSALM 78:38 TPT

God's compassion is a well that will never run dry. He cannot be convinced out of his mercy or talked out of his love. He endlessly forgives; what a hope we've found! He always acts in kindness because his heart is infinitely kind. Why would we stop ourselves from returning to him time and again when his love is better than life itself?

Consider the limitless love of God. Does your mind race with exceptions that you see in your life or in the lives of others? Beloved, there are absolutely no exclusions to his love. Do not be tempted to disqualify yourself because of your mistakes. You will find as you submit to his love over and over again that it is sweeter each time.

God, what can I say about your love? It is almost incomprehensible that I am completely covered by your compassion every single moment of my life. Why would I hold myself back from you? I won't, Lord. Here I am! Cover me again in your unfailing love.

November

Surely you have granted him
unending blessings
and made him glad
with the joy of your presence.

PSALM 21:6 NIV

Held by Mercy

If I say, "My foot slips,"
Your mercy, O LORD, will hold me up.
PSALM 94:18 NKJV

When we consider the rising and setting of the sun, there is something even more predictable than this! We are met with mercy each time we come to our God. It doesn't matter if we fail one time or a thousand, his response is always the same.

Do you struggle to believe that God can forgive you when you repeatedly fail the expectations you set for yourself? It is impossible to exhaust God's tender love. He cannot be convinced out of his affection for you. Whether you find yourself succeeding in life or struggling to get through the day, your Father's kindness toward you is always the same. Let your heart dare to hope that he is as good as he says he is. He will hold you up when you feel like you are falling.

Father of mercy, I won't keep myself from approaching you today. I have to hope that your goodness will not fail me. Even as I tremble at the thought of my own weakness, I ask that you would meet me with the power of your presence. Refine me and make me more like you. I won't stop coming back to you.

Alive in Mercy

Great is your mercy, O Lord;
give me life according to your justice.

PSALM 119:156 NRSV

We were created for so much more than just survival. Life is meant to be full of connection and growth. Where we lack, God fills us. He is the source of everything we need to thrive in this existence. In God's life, we are made alive. His presence within us is what empowers us to love others as he loves us.

We have been brought into fellowship with goodness itself. God's lavish mercy is unending and full of power to all who drink of its waters. We cannot fail when we are hemmed into his unfailing love. As the heavens are high above the earth, so his great love reaches farther than our grasp. May we never lose interest in God's heart of compassion that meets us with abundance.

Lord, you are greater than the highest mountain or the deepest sea. Your mysteries unfold before my eyes and I see glimpses of your goodness in every created thing. When I consider the beauty that is derived from darkness and pressure in the formation of diamonds, how could I question whether you are doing the same in me? Open my eyes to your wondrous ways.

Shine Light

Do everything without grumbling or arguing, so that you may become blameless and pure, "children of God without fault in a warped and crooked generation." Then you will shine among them like stars in the sky as you hold firmly to the word of life.

PHILIPPIANS 2:14-16 NIV

When we surrender our hearts to the Lord, we tether ourselves to his unfailing love. As we live in the place of submission, our lives begin to reflect his perfect nature. In his light, we become light. We reflect the goodness of our Father when we are yielded to his kindness and mercy.

When our resources are running dry and we don't have much buffer of grace, it is good to check in with our connection to God. When was the last time we spent time in his presence being filled by his love? It is impossible to give away what we do not have. God is unending in tender mercy, so let us go to him with our need again and again. It is not failure to need refreshing; unhindered connection is what we were designed for.

God, as your child, I come to you to be reminded of your good nature. I want to spend time in your presence, reawakening to the love that never ends and never changes. Only from this place of being filled up to overflowing can I freely give it away to others.

Alive Together

God, being rich in mercy,
because of His great love with which He loved us,
even when we were dead in our transgressions,
made us alive together with Christ
(by grace you have been saved).
EPHESIANS 2:4-5 NASB

In areas of our lives where we see destruction and devastation, there is hope. We have been made alive with Christ in his resurrection. This means that whatever doesn't look fruitful is awaiting the redemption that God works within and for us. There is no situation too bleak that he cannot bring beauty and regeneration from it.

God is in the business of doing the impossible. What seems out of the question in our minds is an invitation to faith and trust in God's miracle-working power. We have been covered in grace that empowers us. He changes us from the inside out and brings beauty out of the ashes of despair. And he does it again and again! Let us hope in him, for he is surely not finished with us yet.

God, you are so rich in mercy. It is almost incomprehensible that I cannot deplete your love in my life. Thank you for a reality that is more wonderful than my highest hopes. Breathe on the barren parts of my life and heart and bring new life as only you can do.

Persistent Peace

The LORD will fight for you,
and you shall hold your peace.
EXODUS 14:14 NKJV

When situations spiral out of our control and we can't see the way out, God is a firm foundation. He does not change with the shifting winds that send our minds spinning. In him we find our peace, and it's the kind that can't be taken from us. God will fight the battles that we cannot; when we rely on him, we will see that he executed everything perfectly.

Even in the midst of troubles and storms, God is unchanging and we are hidden in him. If God is not shaken, neither will we be. He is our refuge and our strength, and he will not let us be crushed by the weight of our burdens. He fights for us! He will never stop defending his children as long as it is called today.

Lord, fight for me. You see the areas that are completely out of my depth and control; there's nothing I can do to help myself. You are so much wiser than I am. You see it all from the beginning to the end and everything in between. Fill my heart with peace and confidence as I rest in your unfailing love.

Return

Let the wicked forsake their way,
and the unrighteous their thoughts;
let them return to the Lord,
that he may have mercy on them,
and to our God,
for he will abundantly pardon.

ISAIAH 55:7 NRSV

God is a gracious Father. He patiently waits for his children to return to him when they insist on going their own way. When we are lost to our own whims and desires, we will ultimately find that nothing is enough to satisfy the longing of relationship that we have for God. In him we have the goodness that we are looking for.

Have you been trying to find pleasure and fulfillment your own way? There is no time limit to God's mercy. Today is the perfect opportunity to return to your good Father. He welcomes you with open arms whenever you approach. Do not fear his judgment; he is full of love and forgiveness, and he will restore everything back to you. It is not too good to be true—it is his promise.

Merciful Father, I can't begin to thank you for all that you've done for me. Even in my wandering, you love me. I come back to you with my heart wide open. What a relief that you receive me and wash me clean in your love. I am undone in your presence.

Wonderful Grace

His unforgettable works of surpassing wonder
reveal his grace and tender mercy.
PSALM 111:4 TPT

Sometimes when we are holding onto hope, we reduce God's incredible mercy to lofty ideals. The reality of God's goodness is that he tangibly works amazing things in our lives. Where we struggle to see his kindness at work in our lives right now, may we press into his presence until we see through the eyes of his love.

God is a miracle worker. He does what no one else could dream of doing. If there are circumstances in our lives that oppose his compassion, we can be sure that restoration is coming. God specializes in redemption, and he never gives up in love. He is not done with us yet.

Good God, you are more loving than I can imagine. Holy Spirit, meet me in the midst of both my messes and my joys today. I don't want a single moment to go wasted, knowing that you are always working. Entwine my heart with yours so I sense you in everything. Don't stop working in wonderful ways.

Lasting Virtues

Three things will last forever—
faith, hope, and love—
and the greatest of these is love.
1 CORINTHIANS 13:13 NLT

When everything else fades away in life, there are three things that remain unchanged: confident trust based on God's good character and faithfulness, hopeful expectation of the fulfillment of God's promises, and love that conquers all fears.

God's love is greater than any other force known in the heavens or on the earth. It is strong enough to defeat death, powerful enough to make the sick well, and faithful enough to cover every living thing that has ever existed. Where we have been limited in love, may God's mercy meet us in new ways that blow open every box that we put it in. Where we have put boundaries on kindness, let us see today that this is not what God does. His compassion is wider reaching than we could ever comprehend.

Loving God, you are wealthy in love in ways that I try but fail to imagine. Make your mercy more real to me today as I look for you everywhere I go. Give me eyes to see a glimpse of the limitless love you pour out on all. I know that you are better than I give you credit for.

Leaning In

Hear the voice of my pleas for mercy,
when I cry to you for help,
when I lift up my hands toward your most holy sanctuary.

PSALM 28:2 ESV

When we find ourselves in need, it is not a fault. Self-sufficiency is not a fruit of the Spirit, nor is it a requirement of worth. In fact, we find our true identity wrapped up in the love of the Father which never changes and has nothing to do with our circumstances. When we cry out to God, he hears and answers.

Do you feel like a failure when you recognize areas in your life that are lacking? Take a moment today to align to God's perspective. Boldly come to your Father, asking for whatever you need with an unfiltered heart. He won't let you down, and he won't leave you the same. Lean in today to the tender love of your good God.

Good Father, here I am coming to you again. I won't try to dress myself up today or pretend that I'm not hurting. You see my heart so clearly: why do I try to hide from you? Meet me with the power of your mercy that changes me. I rely on you, Lord.

Like Minded

Rejoice, be made complete, be comforted,
be like-minded, live in peace;
and the God of love and peace will be with you.
2 CORINTHIANS 13:11 NASB

When we are living in isolation, everything feels more concentrated. Sadness has nowhere to go but to steep in our souls, and we must rely on our own reserves to get us by. The problem with this is that we were never meant to go it alone. A shared burden is less heavy, and comfort from a friend is priceless.

When we find people we can trust, it takes practice to remain vulnerable enough to share the realities of our hardships. It is important to have people who are leaning into faith along with us; we become like iron, sharpening each other as we live with openness. We will experience God in even deeper ways as we share life with others who are leaning into love.

Father, I see that you have created me for community. Where I am isolated, would you provide safe people with whom I can grow? I don't want to live relying solely on my own strength and resources. I know that I live a limited life if it is not in connection with others. Help me to see how I can be more open.

Kind God

May the Lord show you his kindness
and have mercy on you.
NUMBERS 6:25 NCV

In most religions, gods are not known for their kindness. They are known for power and impossible requirements. But the Lord of all of heaven and earth stands above the rest. He is full of mercy and power. His compassion dictates his interactions with us. He does not require us to be or do anything good on our own. What kind of a God is that?

In goodness, the Lord shows us the tender affections of his heart through the faithfulness of his presence with us. He is not easily angered, and he does not grow impatient with us even though we deserve it by our own standards. God is so much greater. His ways are higher than ours and his motives purer than our best intentions. May our hearts know the fullness of his kindness toward us and never lose hope.

God of kindness, you are so much better than I could ever dream of being. I'm so grateful that you are patient in love and full of mercy toward me every single day. Just when I feel like I have exhausted your goodness, you remind me that you are the same yesterday, today, and forever. Show me your love again, Lord!

No More Walls

*He himself is our peace, who has made us both one
and has broken down in his flesh the dividing wall of hostility.*

EPHESIANS 2:14 ESV

Restoration of connection with the Father has been given to us freely through the sacrifice and power of Jesus' resurrection. Where there was once a wall of hostility raised in our hearts, there is now an openness of relationship. There is nothing that holds us back. Jesus broke down every obstacle that once kept us from knowing God in the fullness of fellowship.

Is there any hostility left within your heart? Invite God into it if you dare. There is nothing that can stand against his strong love; he himself is the one who has done the hard work of restoration. If there is any hesitation in your heart toward the Lord, let his presence bring light to the source.

God of peace, you are so rich in love and mercy. I don't want to resist your love in any area of my life, so lead me into healing and restoration where I lack understanding. I believe that you are better to me than I am to myself. I trust you!

Perfect Peace

"Peace I leave with you; my peace I give to you.
I do not give to you as the world gives.
Do not let your hearts be troubled,
and do not let them be afraid."
JOHN 14:27 NRSV

When fear threatens to send us running from reality, let us take a moment to breathe in the very-present nearness of God. He has not left us to our own survival skills and coping mechanisms. There is a better way. God's peace is like a warm, fragrant breeze in the springtime. It fills us with the awareness of the here and now and the sweetness of the fragrant presence of what is close by. Though we cannot see the Holy Spirit, we know the ways in which he moves.

God does not give like those expecting something in return. Freely he gives; freely let us receive. Peace that transcends our understanding is the peace he gives; it meets us in confusion and brings clarity. It calms the restless heart and brings relief to the stresses that would keep us on edge. He is so good, and his love is more predictable than fear.

Steady One, you are perfect in power, love, and peace. I need you to calm my anxieties and breathe your peace into my body. May I align with the stability of your kindness today. I am yours. Fill me with your peace.

Filled to Overflowing

Look at how much encouragement you've found in your relationship with the Anointed One! You are filled to overflowing with his comforting love. You have experienced a deepening friendship with the Holy Spirit and have felt his tender affection and mercy.

PHILIPPIANS 2:1 TPT

When we submit our lives to God, it is not like servants yielding to a master. It is more like children entrusting themselves to their caring parents. God is full of mercy and love, an ever-present help in times of trouble, and he is full of joyful delight in us.

His comforting love meets us when we need it most. It is an ever-flowing fountain of compassion that does not stop covering us. In friendship with the Holy Spirit, we are able to feel God's kindness and tender care for us. What an amazing relationship! Where others leave us feeling unsatisfied, we find ultimate fulfillment in love that always heals, always restores, and always draws us in.

God of abundance, you are the source of everything good. Your presence awakens me to life over and over again. I am not just filled with enough but filled to overflowing. Do it again, Lord!

Ours in Christ

Grace, mercy and peace will be with us,
from God the Father and from Jesus Christ,
the Son of the Father, in truth and love.

2 JOHN 1:3 NASB

As we walk this earth, we face trials and troubles of many kinds. We can't escape pain, and we can't ignore suffering. It is not a gift of the Spirit to deny the ache of the hurting. This is not how God operates. He is quick to comfort, patient in mercy, and full of kindness to the heartbroken.

Where do you need God's grace to meet you today? Where do you need his peace to flood your life? What area requires his mercy? You can be sure that he meets you with the abundance of his heart today. He freely gives all that you need. Boldly ask him to fill you today; he will not let you down.

Jesus Christ, in you is all truth and love. I will not hold back from you today. Here is my heart, in its laid-bare state just as it is. Come and meet me with the power of your presence and revive me.

Glory Coming

He will take our weak mortal bodies and change them into glorious bodies like his own, using the same power with which he will bring everything under his control.

PHILIPPIANS 3:21 NLT

There is no escaping the mortality of our bodies, though thankfully our ultimate hope is not in our health in this life. When sickness saps our strength and steals our ambition, it can be a difficult adjustment to make. God is our healer, and that is true in every age. Even when he doesn't heal, he is still as good as he ever was.

The fundamental confident expectation of our faith is that God will raise us to everlasting life just as Jesus was raised with a glorified body no longer confined to the mortality of his limited form. We will be changed, once and for all, in his power in the resurrection of our bodies. Whether we are weak or strong now, we will one day be faultless in every way. What a glorious hope.

Holy One, my firm hope is in the coming glory of eternity with you. I know that life now is full of ups and downs, victories and failures, but with you by my side, I can face it all. You empower me to live with hope, and even when that falters, I know that you will never fail.

Set on the Spirit

To set the mind on the flesh is death,
but to set the mind on the Spirit is life and peace.
ROMANS 8:6 ESV

When the worries of life overtake our minds, finding peace within it seems impossible. Despair is not far behind the anxieties that send us spiraling. When we focus on the lack of our circumstances, we will feel as if there is no way out, and the desperation to try and do everything we can to fix it will further deplete our emotional resources.

But there is another way! When we consider the Holy Spirit and the fruit that he so freely gives, we align ourselves with hope and faith. Let us not be drawn into the spiral of unmet needs; rather, let us look to the unchanging character of our good God who never fails. His faithfulness is steady and sure, and we will see the goodness of God in the land of the living. We will see him come through for us again and again.

Ever-present One, thank you for not leaving me to the downward spiral of my anxiety. Holy Spirit, I need you. As I set my heart and thoughts on you, let hope rise again. Breathe peace into my worried heart as I direct my gaze to you. Your faithfulness is sure and you will not let me down. I believe it, Lord.

Led into Truth

"When he, the Spirit of truth, comes,
he will guide you into all the truth."
JOHN 16:13 NIV

When Jesus ascended into heaven, he did not leave us alone. In fact, he clearly told his disciples that it was better that he go so that the Spirit of God could come and minister to all. The Spirit is not confined to a human body, space, or time. He moves freely and widely, dwelling with us in every moment in very tangible ways.

The Holy Spirit illuminates the truth. He leads us into all wisdom. When we are clouded by doubt and confusion, the Spirit brings clarity. What an amazing reality that we have the same Spirit alive within us that raised Christ from the dead! His power, wisdom, and compassion are unrivaled, and he freely gives to all who ask. Let us not stop inviting him into our lives. He is tangible love and wisdom.

Wise One, you lead me along the path of truth. When I start to wander, you bring me back to your love time and again. Don't stop doing it, Holy Spirit. I rely on you for everything I need. You see it all. Meet me where I am and lead me on.

No Wandering

I have tried hard to find you—
don't let me wander from your commands.

PSALM 119:10 NLT

Whether we have spent our whole lives going after God or we have just begun to follow him, the same measure of abundant grace is ours. As we follow after God on the path of love, we will find that when we begin to wander, he gently redirects us.

Are you wondering how you can know if you are wandering from God's ways? Consider the fruit of your life not your bank account, the state of your health, or the success of your career. Look within. What do your thoughts look like? What about the attitude of your heart most days? If you find that you are quick to judge, feeling worthless in love and life, those are clear indicators that you need a realignment in love. He who is full of mercy will meet you with the abundance of his heart today.

Merciful God, I submit my heart to yours again today. Where I am depleted of compassion, fill me with the kindness of your heart. I cannot continue to choose love in my own strength, but I know that you empower me as you freely fill me with your mercy. Thank you, God.

Persistent Grace

*In Your great mercy You did not
utterly consume them nor forsake them;
For You are God, gracious and merciful.*

NEHEMIAH 9:31 NKJV

When we encounter God's amazing mercy in our lives, we cannot deny his goodness. We may have heard of his great compassion before, but until we experience it for ourselves, it simply sounds like a nice idea. We were made for relationship and knowing God has never been about intellectually consuming philosophies. We are whole beings with real needs that God meets with his very real provisions.

God's presence is made manifest in the Holy Spirit, and the Spirit ministers to all who call on the name of the Lord. This includes you! If you haven't experienced the love of God beyond the confines of your mind, invite the Spirit to minister to your heart with his tangible presence. He will fill, empower, and graciously meet you. Your entire being was always meant to be wholly brought into fellowship with him.

God, you are full of grace to all who look for it. In the power of your presence, meet me today with more than the changing of thoughts. Fill my entire being with your love. I want to know the tangible power of your presence in my life.

But God

I had said in my alarm,
"I am cut off from your sight."
But you heard the voice of my pleas for mercy
when I cried to you for help.

PSALM 31:22 ESV

When all seems to be right in our little world and the sun is shining bright, it is easy to recognize the blessing and favor of the Lord. In circumstances where we can't escape the suffering and pain that life sends our way, it is almost second nature to question how God could change so drastically. However, the Word is clear that God is unchanging in love and mercy. His tender kindness is never uncertain.

When we are faced with tragedy, how does it influence our view of God? Do we think that somehow he has forgotten us? He never wavers in compassion, and his thoughts toward us are full of delight in who we are no matter the circumstance. Where our experiences are not matching up with God's character, may we cry out for his goodness to break through. He will never leave us hanging; his mercy meets us at every juncture.

Lord, you are never changing in your perfect nature. When I am struggling to see your goodness at work in my life, come close and fill me with your perspective. Give me the peace of your presence and the mercy of your heart. I rely on you today and forever.

At Peace

If while we were still enemies, God fully reconciled us to himself through the death of his Son, then something greater than friendship is ours. Now that we are at peace with God, and because we share in his resurrection life, how much more we will be rescued from sin's dominion!

ROMANS 5:10 TPT

God's peace is so much richer than the temporary calm we feel when all seems to be right with the world. His peace reaches into the chaos and brings order. It speaks to the storms that are raging and brings complete tranquility. Even when seas still churn around us, he gives us stillness and clarity within.

We could never earn God's acceptance or love; it is ours. It always has been! God's intentions are full of goodness, love, and mercy. His joy is unrivaled, meeting us when we need it most. We are not just counted as God's friends but as his own children; we are a part of his everlasting kingdom. When our hearts begin to falter, may his resurrection power raise us back to life.

Great God, your peace is unlike anything I've experienced. It brings clarity of mind and wisdom even in the harshest of circumstances. It stills the chaos of my mind and fills my body with rest. I am safe in your constant love, and this is my portion forever. Come near, Lord, in the peace of your presence.

Spirit Powered

May the God of hope fill you with all joy and peace in believing,
so that you will abound in hope by the power of the Holy Spirit.

ROMANS 15:13 NASB

Joy is not a side effect of normal living at the pace we are going in this world. Peace is not a natural reaction to the chaos that is everywhere around us. These values are both cultivated and given through fellowship with God. The more time we spend in his presence, the more peace and joy become a part of the fabric of our beings. We learn what it is to walk in love with hope as our vision.

What do you lack today? God is the source of every good thing. May he fill you with everything you need to believe; his faithfulness will supply every necessity. Don't hesitate to press into his presence every time you remember to. He does not disappoint and he won't ever grow tired of your attention.

Ever-present One, you are as vital to me as the air in my lungs. I rely on you for more than strength to go on, but for every good thing in this life. Your joy is unmatched and your peace is beyond comprehension. You are so, so good. Envelop me in your love again today as I rest in you.

Abundantly Blessed

God is able to bless you abundantly,
so that in all things at all times,
having all that you need,
you will abound in every good work.

2 CORINTHIANS 9:8 NIV

Thank God that we are not destined to lives of "just enough." We were never meant to struggle to get by, and God does not give like a stingy old miser. There is always room for more, both in the asking and the receiving. Whatever season of life we find ourselves in, God's abilities are always bigger than our own. Will we trust him?

Take a look around your life and spot the areas that are going well. What are they? Now consider the areas that you are struggling in; is there room for God's power to be at work in every part? His strength is made perfect in weakness. He has wise strategies that will transform even the bleakest situation. Spend time in his presence today and be filled with his abundant love and mercy that will change you from the inside out.

Provider, you are rich in mercy and lovingkindness. Out of the abundance of your heart you give to all who have need. See my needs, Lord. They are plain before you. I won't stop asking for your hand of goodness to be on my life so I may run after you all of my days.

A Better Way

Judgment will be without mercy to anyone who has shown no mercy; mercy triumphs over judgment.

JAMES 2:13 NRSV

Mercy is the way of the cross. When we follow Jesus, we see there is no other way to live like him unless we are choosing to continually live in love. That sounds easy, right? It is surely the more costly way. When we lay down our lives in love, we forgive instead of seeking revenge, we are kind to those who ridicule us, and we sacrifice our own comfort for the truth.

Love is not some flighty ideal but a grounded surrendering. But it is the better way! God's Word says that we will be judged according to how we judge. That should bring us pause. Are we living with mercy as our covering, or are we keeping love at a distance by judging others continuously?

Merciful God, you are the way, the truth, and the life. As I live in your example, I will find the fullness of my life is in you. Help me to choose kindness instead of harsh criticism. May my heart remain humble in your love as I learn to let go of my own hurt and rejection.

Confident Approach

Let us then with confidence draw near to the throne of grace,
that we may receive mercy and find grace to help in time of need.
HEBREWS 4:16 ESV

In the family of God, there are no black sheep. The Father's love is pure and welcoming to each in the same measure of abundant tenderness. If we have been welcomed into his family, there is no reason to hesitate to come to him. He will not ridicule our questions or brush off our pain. Our good God is perfect in compassion and love that satisfies in every condition of the soul.

When was the last time you boldly approached God? Have you been coming to him with confidence, or have you been cautiously circling his table of plenty? You are not meant to pick up the crumbs of others' portions. There is a place reserved for you with everything that will satisfy you piled high, waiting for you to take your place.

Good Father, I will not hesitate to approach your throne of grace today. Here I come, all of me, trusting that you will receive me just as I am. Here at your table of plenty I will eat until I am satisfied. Give me everything I need for the day and more. You are the only one who turns ashes into beauty, and I trust you!

He Is Better

To the LORD our God belong mercy and forgiveness,
though we have rebelled against Him.
DANIEL 9:9 NKJV

God is full of forgiveness. That is a statement that could be meditated on every day for the rest of our lives, and we still wouldn't reach the end of its power or significance. God is not a one-time giver of mercy. He does not have a limit to his love, and he doesn't have a threshold to his forgiveness. We cannot weary him with our failures. Even if we could, he would still choose to show us kindness.

The world does not know this kind of generous love. It is a foreign concept to most. Even to those of us who live yielded to his great compassion, are we not surprised by the depths of his mercy time and again? We could never reach the end of it; what a glorious mystery. May the eyes of our hearts be enlightened to see him as he is today—perfect in love, power, and full of glory!

God, your love is better than anything I've ever known. It never withdraws, always flows toward me, and lifts me up every time I fall. Though I frequently disappoint myself, I find time and again that I haven't disappointed you which is a marvelous mystery. Fill me with the light of your love again today.

Profound Wisdom

If you are truly wise,
you'll learn from what I've told you.
It's time for you to consider these profound lessons
of God's great love and mercy.

PSALM 107:43 TPT

When we are growing up, we learn from trial and error, but we also learn by following the example of trusted people in our lives. True wisdom is found in following the pure example of God's mercy. It's a sure bet that when we align our lives with his unfailing love, we will be found in him.

When we spend time in the presence of God, we cannot help but soak up his goodness. We reflect the nature of the ones we spend most of our time with. What are we filling our time with? Even in the background of our lives, what we give our attention to is what feeds our thoughts and hearts. Let us be thoughtful in our time and intentional with what we consume.

God, when I look back over my life and see what you have done, I am amazed. There is no end to your kindness and tender mercy. As I remember who you have been, meet me in this present moment and do a new thing. You are rich in love, and I am rich in you.

God's Mouthpiece

*The LORD reached out his hand
and touched my mouth and said to me,
"I have put my words in your mouth."*

JEREMIAH 1:9 NIV

Words matter. Anyone in relationship knows that this is true. Words can build up or they can tear down. Are we purposeful in the words we choose? Do we consider what we will say before we speak, especially in times of vulnerability, or do we let words spill from the overflow of our minds and hearts in instant reaction?

When we submit our lives to God, this includes our minds and our mouths. We won't always get it right, and that's where mercy comes in. When our speech is peace-loving and courageously honest while maintaining compassion, we can know that we are reflecting God's character in our approach. We show his nature when we choose humility, mercy, and kindness. May we reflect him in this way.

Lord, touch my lips and make me clean. I know that as I spend time with you, relating to you in your unmatched mercy, that I won't be able to stop myself from showing your nature. And when I don't, I will walk in the way of humility, asking for forgiveness. Fill me that I may pour out to others.

Empowered

May he give you the power to accomplish
all the good things your faith prompts you to do.
2 Thessalonians 1:11 NLT

When we are full of faith, our intentions are set high on being living sacrifices for God. When we feel good, it is so much easier to say, "Yes, Lord!" with willing hearts. When our realities shift and suffering lasts for longer than we had hoped, what then? Do we give up and decide that we are disqualified? Or do we keep persevering in faith even when it feels impossible and, perhaps, pointless?

Thankfully, the requirement of faithfully following God is not our own stamina or abilities. Perseverance is found in continuing to choose to press into God even (and especially) when we feel completely weak and unworthy. The Holy Spirit is our source for strength. He empowers us to keep going, and he fills us with all that we need to not just survive but to thrive. May we turn our attention to him today and be filled afresh.

Holy Spirit, you are the source of everything I need. I yield my heart to yours, knowing that your unfailing love meets me at every single turn. Invade the moments of my day with your tangible grace that strengthens me to do all that you would have me do.

December

On the day I called you,
you answered me.
You made me strong and brave.

PSALM 138:3 NCV

Invited

"Now you should go and study the meaning of the verse:
I want you to show mercy, not just offer me a sacrifice.
For I have come to invite the outcasts of society and sinners,
not those who think they are already on the right path."

MATTHEW 9:13 TPT

Jesus was a perfect reflection of the heart of the Father. When he invited the sick, weak, and broken into his sphere, he clearly showed that God welcomes in those who the world shuts out. There are no outcasts in the kingdom, only members of the same family, all with the same dignity and worth.

Whether you feel acceptable or not within society, God is for you. It does not matter if you measure up to the world's standards. God welcomes you with the love of a tender father. His compassionate heart is turned toward you in affection. Lay down your defenses and come to him, he is waiting to receive you with open arms.

God, I come to you with an open heart looking for belonging. I know that I will find it in you. Meet me with the power of your love that calms every fear. I am covered in your mercy.

Kept in Love

Keep yourselves in the love of God,
waiting for the mercy of our Lord Jesus Christ
that leads to eternal life.

JUDE 1:21 ESV

In the chaos of this world, it can be difficult to remain at peace. There are endless things competing for our attention; how do we rein it all in and focus our thoughts on what matters most? If the threat of anxiety is a constant battle, there are surely areas in our lives that need reprioritizing.

When we are kept in the mercy of God that surrounds us, fears are calmed. The presence of God envelops us with his love and we find the stillness of confidence that leads us to rest. When the pace of life just won't quit, may we practice slowing ourselves down and setting boundaries on our time and attention. As we do this, even the mundane feels more meaningful.

Loving God, you constantly surround me with the embrace of your compassion. Do not leave me to my own whims, Lord. I want to find rest in the peace of your presence. Teach me as I take steps to walk in wisdom.

Strength to Stand

Your words have comforted those who fell,
and you have strengthened those who could not stand.

JOB 4:4 NCV

God is a support to the weak and strength to the wavering. He never requires us to rely on our own abilities in life, not even on our best days. In our frailty, God's power is perfectly shown off. We can never veer too far off the path of his love that he cannot bring us back. We are kept in love even when we wander.

When sorrow saps every emotional reserve we have, we can't even stand on our own. In these moments, the Comforter comes closer than we've known and camps in the battlefield of our hearts. He binds the broken parts and tends to the wounds. He leaves no part untouched by his unfailing love. He makes a dwelling place within us and does his restorative work.

God of my comfort, come close with your presence. You don't require me to stand or to do anything. You meet me in my pain and suffering and you go to work healing and tending to me. You are too wonderful for words. Don't ever stop your beautiful work in my heart.

Increased Honor

You will increase my honor,
and comfort me once again.
PSALM 71:21 NRSV

Our worth is found in the one who has given us life. We don't need to earn even a portion of our honor. He freely offers dignity to all, not missing anyone. What a tremendous relief it is that he is the giver of our inherent worth. God, who is kind in nature, merciful, and forever compassionate, is the one who esteems us as his own children. With a father like that, we couldn't ever lose our dignity to another; even if we did, he would restore it.

The one who gives us our value is the one who also increases our honor. With our lives woven into his, we cannot help but reflect the goodness of his nature. He is perfectly peaceful and wonderfully kind. May we not lose heart when we falter and fail, for even then we are covered by his mercy.

Lord, you are the lifter of my head and my firm foundation.
I find my true identity wrapped up in your presence: in your
light, I see more clearly. Thank you for loving me. I cannot
begin to deserve your endless kindness toward me.

Sing for Joy

Sing for joy, O heavens, and exult, O earth;
break forth, O mountains, into singing!
For the LORD has comforted his people,
and will have compassion on his suffering one.

ISAIAH 49:13 NRSV

When we are under the weight of suffocating circumstances that don't seem to change as we cry out for help, may God's comfort meet us and lift the weight of the burden. His compassion is not absent from anything we go through. May he draw near in kindness and bring peace with his presence.

The birds cannot stop singing, and the winds have their own song. Why would we hold ours back when God's mercy is clearly at hand? Let us lift our songs to the Lord: in rejoicing, in surrender, in awe, and in the waiting. He is always worthy! Though we change, he never does.

God, you are always worthy of the praise I offer you, yet you don't demand it from me. You are kind in your patience. What a wonderful God you are. I present my heart to you today, and I lift my voice as an offering of gratitude. You are so, so good!

Ready Relief

You who are my Comforter in sorrow,
my heart is faint within me.
JEREMIAH 8:18 NIV

God of the angel armies, who wars on behalf of the vulnerable, is the same God who draws close to the brokenhearted. He lifts the burdens of the weary and carries the weak into places of rest. He has never turned away from a wounded soul looking for reprieve. He is the strength that brings respite to the tired and liberation to the tied down.

Is your heart in need of relief today? May God draw close to you in your place of need. He never misses the mark. May his unfailing love flood your heart, mind, and body. He satisfies with his mercy, and he won't leave you wanting. Where you are looking for help, may God answer you quickly and clearly in his wisdom.

Comforter, in your arms I find the relief I am looking for. Your love ministers to my heart in ways that I can't even put into words. Thank you for your mercy that never leaves me. I rely on you for the wisdom I need. Come in power again.

Thread of Faithfulness

My loving God, the harp in my heart will praise you.
Your faithful heart toward us
will be the theme of my song.
Melodies and music will rise to you,
the Holy One of Israel.

PSALM 71:22 TPT

Everything that God does is done with faithfulness as the thread holding it all together. He creates tapestries out of the cords of our lives. What he does is beautiful and far beyond our understanding. His love is stitched into the fabric of our lives. When we look back, we see that he has been working all along. There is no place that his redemption leaves untouched.

When you look back over your life, where do you see God's love at work even when you were completely unaware of it at the time? Do you see his fingerprints on your story? If you're struggling to see where he was, take a moment in his presence and ask for his perspective. Ask him to show you where he was. He is faithful to answer.

Loving God, your faithfulness is woven into my life. Give me eyes to see where you were in areas I thought were untouched by you. I submit my heart to yours, knowing that you are kind, gentle, and for me. Speak, Lord.

Weary Comforted

The Sovereign LORD has given me his words of wisdom,
so that I know how to comfort the weary.
Morning by morning he wakens me
and opens my understanding to his will.

ISAIAH 50:4 NLT

God's wisdom is given for all to understand. Those who seek his guidance will find it; his perfect nature does not go back on any of his promises. Those who seek him will find him; those who mourn will be comforted. Those who hope in him will not be disappointed. What a wonderful God!

As we spend time in God's Word and in his presence, he gives us the revelation light of understanding that opens our hearts and minds to his perfect ways. The length of his love no one can fathom. There is no beginning and no end to his mercy. May our hearts grow in confidence of his perfect love as we soak it in more and more every day.

Holy One, you offer unending kindness to those who come to you. Fill me with the understanding of your goodness and your wonderful character as I look to you. There is no one else like you.

Never Left

"Blessed are the poor in spirit,
for theirs is the kingdom of heaven.
Blessed are those who mourn,
for they will be comforted."

MATTHEW 5:3-4 NIV

God is a constant source of comfort in the midst of our suffering. He does not leave us in our pain, and he certainly doesn't turn away from us in our desperation. He is always with us. He comforts the mourning, strengthens the weak, and offers hope to the heartbroken. His love never fails.

What does it mean to you that God will never abandon you? It doesn't matter what you're facing; God is with you in every moment. Right where you are, in whatever circumstances you are up against, God is there! Take heart. He is near.

God of all comfort, I cling to you today. Even when my voice cracks and I can't form words, there you are in complete understanding. Holy Spirit, come closer as I turn my attention to you.

Father of Mercies

Blessed be the God and Father of our Lord Jesus Christ, the Father of mercies and God of all comfort, who comforts us in all our affliction so that we will be able to comfort those who are in any affliction with the comfort with which we ourselves are comforted by God.

2 CORINTHIANS 1:3-4 NASB

When we are overcome by the burdens of life, there is someone we can turn to who is closer than a brother. God, the Father of all mercy and the greatest comforter, is a safe place we can run into. There is no better friend we will find.

Every struggle and every sorrow we experience is a place where God offers relief and consolation. There is no burden too big that he stays away. There is nothing that intimidates the Lord, and there is no shame too heavy that he will not lift it. As we are comforted by his tender care, we are able to offer this same kind of comfort to others.

Father, you are faithful in lovingkindness. Your tenderness is reassuring to my weary soul. When I can barely stand, you hold me. Thank you for never leaving me; your constant presence is life to me.

Unbiased God

The LORD wants to show his mercy to you.
He wants to rise and comfort you.
The LORD is a fair God,
and everyone who waits for his help will be happy.

ISAIAH 30:18 NCV

God's love cannot be exhausted by our questioning. His patience is much longer than our own. He welcomes us even with our hesitations about his character. Our doubts won't last long in the presence of God, but even if they did, they would not diminish his power.

God's love welcomes each of us with the openness of his eager heart. He does not give in one measure to some and to others more or less. He gives equally to all. When we wait for his help, we will not be disappointed. He comforts us as we rest in him. His nearness is so rich. We can't help but be loved to life by him over and over again.

Lord, you are amazing in your unbiased nature. I'm thankful that you don't look at me the way the world does. You see each person as worthy of your unending love. I am worthy of love because you have said that I am. I lean into your heart again today.

Born into Hope

All you who put your hope in the Lord
be strong and brave.

PSALM 31:24 NCV

When we are lacking in hope, where do we go to find perspective? Spending too much time focused on our troubles can cause anxiety to rise as we consider our lack of options. But God is full of miracle-working power; he also has much clearer perspective than we do.

In Christ we have a hope that cannot be diminished. He has given us new life in his resurrection power. We no longer need to fear death or its consequences. There is so much anticipation in the glory that awaits us. Eternal life without pain, suffering, or limitations is ours through Jesus. He is forever kind, full of mercy, and he covers us in compassion—both now and forever.

Jesus, you are the hope that I cling to in the long days of waiting. There is no one as wonderful as you. I am so grateful to have been born into your kingdom. Thank you for mercy that covers me every moment of my life. Awaken my heart to the hope I have in you.

Sincere Wisdom

The wisdom from above is first pure, then peaceable, gentle,
open to reason, full of mercy and good fruits, impartial and sincere.

JAMES 3:17 ESV

The wisdom of God is full of pure motives. He does not have a hidden agenda. Wisdom is peace-loving and gentle, causing people to consider a better way. There is kindness inherent in the revelation that God gives; the fruit of it cannot be mistaken. It is genuine and unbiased, not being easily swayed. God's perfect nature is evident in the wisdom that he gives in his Word.

When you are looking for guidance, where do you turn? How do you know what kind of advice to take? Submit your plans to God, and he will direct you. You will know that it is wisdom guiding you when it is full of the characteristics of God's nature. Don't overcomplicate it; he is faithful to help you.

Wise One, you are the source of every answer I'm looking for. I know that you won't disappoint me as I follow you. I need you more than I know how to express. Fill me with your love as I surrender my mind to you today.

Better than Sacrifice

*I desire mercy and not sacrifice,
And the knowledge of God more than burnt offerings.*

HOSEA 6:6 NKJV

God's requirements are vastly different than the demands we place on ourselves. In a world of endless to-do lists, we are constantly fighting the strain that this kind of pace requires. When we push to require more of ourselves and others, God encourages mercy. Compassion is the way of the Lord.

When we approach God, is it with all of our accomplishments in our back pockets, ready to let him know what we're doing for him? Or do we come to him with humble hearts longing for connection? He never turns away a hungry heart; doing great things for the Lord isn't the point of relationship with him. It is not worthless, but it is not where we find our worth.

Merciful God, I know that in knowing you, I will become more like you. Help me to be as gracious with myself as you are. Give me a tender heart for those around me as well, so I have compassion for them instead of criticism. Your way of mercy is so much better than my way of storing up achievements.

Show Me

Magnify the marvels of your mercy to all who seek you.
Make your Pure One wonderful to me,
like you do for all those who turn aside
to hide themselves in you.

PSALM 17:7 TPT

There is no safer place to find ourselves than in the heart of God. When we hide ourselves in him, his beauty surrounds us. God's mercy is a covering to all who come to him. We cannot stay on the outside of his love when he rushes quickly to meet us as we approach him.

We will see God's goodness as we spend time soaking in his presence. It is pure life to the thirsty soul. Every lack we find within ourselves is filled in the outflow of God's mercy. He is so good! As we gaze upon him, his kindness is exemplified in our hearts.

Great God, you are so abundant in mercy. Let me see more of your glory than I've ever seen before. Your goodness surrounds me, of that I'm sure. Give me eyes to see you all around and encourage my heart to hope as I hide myself in your love.

Present Peace

May the Lord of peace himself give you peace
at all times and in every way.
The Lord be with all of you.
2 Thessalonians 3:16 NIV

The peace of God is no small thing. It is not a consolation prize, and it is not a vain longing. When we have peace, we are dwelling in the stillness of his heart. We don't need to wait until the chaos of our lives subsides to experience this perfect peace. He calms every storm, and he can certainly calm the storms of our hearts so we experience confident trust.

Today is the perfect opportunity to invite the presence of God to dwell within us, calming every anxiety and stilling every worry. His presence is always with us. There are no conditions under which we are outside of his mercy and grace. Where we would keep ourselves in cycles of shame and chaos, may we yield our hearts instead to his embrace.

God of peace, you are my perfect portion. In every moment your love is available. I submit my heart to you again, giving you full access. Breathe your peace into my soul, calming my busy mind. May I live with your peace actively sustaining and revitalizing my being.

Freed from Fear

I prayed to the LORD, and he answered me.
He freed me from all my fears.
Those who look to him for help will be radiant with joy.

PSALM 34:4-5 NLT

There is no promise God makes that will not be fulfilled. He is faithful. He is present. We can be sure that when we pray and seek him, he will answer. Do we trust his character? When he answers differently than we expect, will we write off his goodness, or will we reconsider what it looks like?

God is full of love, and perfect love pushes out every fear. Where worry and dread have stopped us in our tracks, God is faithful to come and pull us out of the sludge. He frees us! Let us look to him even when the waiting feels long. He has not given up or let go of us. May today be the day we experience the breakthrough of liberty, filling us with joy.

Faithful One, your love never leaves us. Meet me in the middle of the doubts and fears that swirl around my mind. I cannot make the wrong things right, but I know that you can. Free me from all my worries as I look to you. You are the one I depend on. I have no other hope.

Healed by Mercy

I have seen what they have done,
but I will heal them.
I will guide them and comfort them
and those who felt sad for them.
They will all praise me.

ISAIAH 57:18 NCV

When we consider the character of God, we cannot escape his faithfulness. His goodness is on display for all to see. Who is like him? He fully sees every wrong done, every selfish ambition, every evil intent, yet he is not marred by such things. He sees everything clearly, and still he chooses to act in love.

God heals us not because we deserve it, but because it reflects his good nature. Even in our rebellion, we cannot convince God to stop loving us. He is the God of a thousand chances; there is no limit to his love. He promises to guide and comfort us through this life. How could our response be anything but gratitude? Even if it's not, he does not change his strategy.

Merciful God, thank you for your leadership in my life.
I submit my heart again to yours today. Heal me, Lord,
of all my sickness. Restore the seeping wounds of my heart.
I am yours.

The Merciful Way

*"If you had known what this means,
'I desire mercy, and not sacrifice,'
you would not have condemned the guiltless."*

MATTHEW 12:7 ESV

God's requirements are so different than ours. He does not demand perfection, nor does he expect us to drive ourselves into the ground by working. He is full of mercy, compassion, and kindness. The weak and vulnerable are not degraded in his presence. They are welcomed in and covered by love.

When we consider our intentions in interactions with our friends, family, and even strangers, what is the fruit of it? Are we living in order to keep up appearances? When it comes down to it, the only obligation we have is that of love. When we choose to walk in the way of mercy, it will change us. We will reflect the character of our good God.

Merciful One, you are a mystery to the world's ways and systems. You do not require success or perfection in order to be worth anything. My worth is found in you, and it always has been. I want to look like you in love. Fill me with your fiery presence that burns away every bad intention. In your kindness, I have found mercy to give away. Thank you, Lord.

Posture of Waiting

By the help of your God, return;
Observe mercy and justice,
And wait on your God continually.

HOSEA 12:6 NKJV

When life gets hectic and we are caught up in the never-ending demands of family, work, and societal expectations, how do we slow down? It is not reasonable that we would work ourselves to the bone for a to-do list that keeps growing. God did not design us for burnout but for partnership with him. We find true rest when we train our souls to wait on him even in the chaos.

When we turn (and return) our hearts to the Lord, we are practicing the intentional submission of ourselves to God. As we live with mercy and justice as deep values, we are already aligned with his character. We can't help but be changed by him when we are living connected to his heart.

God, I surrender my heart to yours again. Teach me to wait continually on you as I go about my day. You are the strength of my life. Your love is my resolve. Be my help when I get caught up in the chaos. Bring the peace of your presence as I wait on you.

Abundant Love

*Our fathers who were delivered from Egypt
didn't fully understand your wonders,
and they took you for granted.
Over and over you showed them
such tender love and mercy!
Yet they were barely beyond the Red Sea
when they rebelled against you.*

PSALM 106:7 TPT

When we take God for granted, he does not fail to show up in love and mercy. He is not easily angered, and he cannot be convinced to abandon compassion. God's character is not dependent on our own. He abounds in kindness even in our rebellion.

Have you been avoiding God because you fear he will be disappointed in your choices? Do you fear that he will punish you and turn away? Though others may abandon you, God will never do it. There is nothing you can do, nothing you can say, nowhere you can go that you can outrun his incredible love. He is always ready to receive you with his tender mercy. He will take the ashes of destruction and make something beautiful.

Father, you are so full of love and mercy. I bring you my heart and all I've kept hidden for fear that you would punish me. I know that you are better than the kindest person I've known, and I trust your heart. Even as I come trembling, I offer you everything again.

Beginning and End

*"I am the Alpha and the Omega—
the Beginning and the End.
To all who are thirsty I will give freely
from the springs of the water of life."*
REVELATION 21:6 NLT

It is difficult to imagine someone without beginning or end. As finite people living in a world with clear inceptions and endings, it is almost too much to comprehend eternity. God, the source of all life, has given us hope in his everlasting nature. Though we cannot grasp the lengths of his love, we can continually grow in our understanding of it as he gives us glimpses throughout our lives.

What a wonderful gift we have in the Holy Spirit. He has all wisdom, and he freely gives revelations of God's perfect nature to those who are looking. We will not be disappointed when we find that his kindness and comfort really does keep on going. What a wonder that we cannot exhaust his love.

Good God, you are the source of all that is pure and true. As I come to you today, fill me with fresh revelation that enlivens my heart and encourages my soul. You are always flowing, never receding, in compassion. Even if I stopped coming to you, you would never give up on me. You are incomparably wonderful.

Defender and Refuge

I will sing of Your power;
Yes, I will sing aloud of Your mercy in the morning;
For You have been my defense
And refuge in the day of my trouble.

PSALM 59:16 NKJV

God is defender of the weak and a place of safety for the vulnerable. When was the last time you felt the frailty of your humanity? God's power is made perfect in your weakness. He is the strength you need at every moment. When you cannot go on in your own strength, when your motivation wanes, he will refresh you in the power of his presence.

Sometimes, all we can do is run into the shelter of the Most High. Other times, we are carried into his presence when our legs buckle under the weight of suffering. We were never meant to crawl through life barely surviving. We were created to thrive; he restores and revives us from the inside out. Where we are struggling to keep going, let us find the rest we need in the shelter of our God. His mercy never fails.

God, you are my refuge. I hide myself in you as you pour your mercy over my life. I need your presence as much as I ever have. Thank you that I need never face any challenge or situation on my own. You are the strength of my life and the encourager of my weary heart.

Steadfast Love

Be mindful of your mercy, O Lord,
and of your steadfast love,
for they have been from of old.
PSALM 25:6 NRSV

The loyal love of God is not a new concept. It was not a new value when Jesus appeared on the scene. God's unwavering, persistent compassion and mercy have always been consistently present. They make up who God is, and he does not change.

God acts in kindness; he always has. Where we have misunderstood his character and wrongly accused his intentions, may we have heavenly perspective to see what has always been true. In humility, we offer God our lives, inviting him into every part. We can trust him because he is good. He does not need to be reminded of his character; it is for our benefit. May we stir up faith as we consider his faithfulness.

Lord, you have always been full of lovingkindness. Retrain my eyes to see your goodness where I have felt confusion over your character. I know that you never fail. Where things don't line up, I know that it is because I do not see the bigger picture. I yield my heart to yours again and trust your faithfulness to lead me on.

God With Us

"Look! The virgin will conceive a child!
She will give birth to a son,
and they will call him Immanuel,
which means 'God is with us.'"

MATTHEW 1:23 NLT

God with us: what a wonderful gift from heaven! When Jesus came to earth, he set the tone for our new reality. We have not been left on our own or to our own devices. God is present with us. What a glorious miracle! Where we have been discouraged in our lives, may we clearly see the nearness of our Savior.

We have been welcomed into God's family, which is wonderfully inclusive. Where we have felt isolated and alone, may we be drawn into the heart of our ever-close God through the Spirit. There is no sadness too great that his comfort cannot touch it. Where there is sorrow and loss, God meets us right in the middle of it. We need not dress ourselves up and pretend that it doesn't exist. Where we are, there he is.

Immanuel, you continually meet me with your presence. Jesus, you are the fulfillment of the promises of the Father. Thank you for your Spirit that loves me to life again and again. I honor you, and I remember today that you are closer than my mother or father. Thank you!

Path of Peace

*"Because of God's tender mercy,
the morning light from heaven is about to break upon us,
to give light to those who sit in darkness
and in the shadow of death,
to guide us to the path of peace."*

LUKE 1:78-79 NLT

God guides us in tender mercy. The way of the Lord is full of peace, kindness, and grace. They are the most powerful forces on earth, though apart from God they tend to sound weak. What a wonder that the wisdom of God is so different from the wisdom of man. Where in this world power equals force and influence, Jesus demonstrated God's power through humility.

As we follow God, he leads us into the way of peace. Our hearts find rest in his unfailing love, and this perfect peace cannot be taken away by anyone or anything. It is the gift of God, given by and through the Holy Spirit who is faithfully with us. May the Son of Righteousness shine his light on us and lead us into stillness.

Holy One, I come to you with all of my messiness today. Shine your light of love on me and lead me into rest. I trust you to guide me to your way of peace because you know the way. I don't rely on my own understanding but on your wisdom which supersedes mine. Your way is better.

Hope of the Helpless

Lord, you know the hopes of the helpless.
Surely you will hear their cries and comfort them.

PSALM 10:17 NLT

God is undisturbed by the troubles that surround us even as he meets us in our weakness. He weeps with those who weep and he heals the broken; he is never dissuaded from his promises or overcome with defeat. He is the victorious one. Next to him, no one measures up!

The all-powerful, all-knowing God is the same one who is full of mercy to the broken and hurting. He rushes to our rescue with the comfort of his presence. He is not slow in keeping his promises. His timeline takes more than our limited understanding into consideration. He is always on time. Let us take heart that he sees, knows, and meets us where we are.

God of my hope, all of my expectations lie in you. You are the giver of good gifts and your presence is the most amazing one. Draw nearer as I cry out to you. Be my comfort and my strength. You're all I have!

Time to Look

Sow for yourselves righteousness;
Reap in mercy;
Break up your fallow ground,
For it is time to seek the Lord,
Till He comes and rains righteousness on you.

HOSEA 10:12 NKJV

There is wisdom to be found when we look for it. There is understanding awaiting us as we ask God for his revelation light to shine in our minds. As we seek him, he draws closer to us. His ways are marked by unfailing love and unending mercy. His kindness, who can top? There is no one in the world who is more patient in compassion than our gracious God.

Let us not grow tired of looking to the Lord. He is always near and always ready to help. He faithfully rains his love over us, covering us with his presence that brings life. Now is all we are given; this moment is our opportunity. May we turn our attention to him more and more!

Lord, I look to you today. You are the keeper of my soul and the hope of my entire life. As I turn my attention to you, come close and speak your words of life. Rain your righteousness over me today.

Not Overwhelmed

The name of the Lord is blessed and lifted high!
For his marvelous miracle of mercy protected me
when I was overwhelmed by my enemies.

PSALM 31:21 TPT

God's mercy is truly a miracle. Even in our attempts to understand it, do we not need to be reminded over and over again of the limitless levels of it? Our minds cannot contain the fullness of the compassion and kindness of the heart of our Good Father. We are carried by his mercy in our triumphs and our defeat. In weakness, he is our strength. He is the defender of our souls. He will not let us fall beyond his grip.

Let today be the day we give him our trust again. When we are overwhelmed, there he is, right in the middle of it all. He breathes peace into our chaos, calming every storm. There is nothing too messy that he cannot clean up. There is no situation too confusing that his wisdom doesn't set straight. His ways never fail.

Merciful God, you are the one who holds me steady throughout the seasons of life. There is no situation too difficult for you to handle. I lean into your understanding. Cover me in your mercy and protect me when I am overwhelmed. As always, I depend on you.

In the Valley

Even though I walk through the darkest valley,
I will fear no evil, for you are with me;
your rod and your staff, they comfort me.

PSALM 23:4 NIV

Whatever we face in this world, we do it with the constant companionship of a good God. He is always with us. When we walk through dark valleys of suffering, he is with us even then. We can't escape his presence even if we try. We need not fear what lurks in the shadows with God, our present help and protector, leading us through the valley. Everything is as clear as day to him.

Knowing that we are led by a Good Shepherd, our hearts can take rest in the comfort of his guidance. His wisdom never falters. What a glorious hope we have. When our faith wavers, may our hearts be strengthened by the presence of the Holy Spirit who ministers to us.

Good Shepherd, you are the leader of my life. In your love I find the comfort that I need and the joy that I long for. There is no one else like you who is perfect in mercy and a constant giver of peace. You are my portion. Lead me on as I lean on you today.

All Things New

He who sits on the throne said, "Behold, I am making all things new."
And He said, "Write, for these words are faithful and true."

REVELATION 21:5 NASB

The King of heaven and earth is faithful and true. Abounding in love, never-ending in mercy, he freely gives to all who come to him. What looks like an end to us is an opportunity for new life in the hands of our masterful Maker. He never quits, and he is not discouraged.

As you prepare for a new year, consider the nearness of your merciful God who never leaves you. He is with you in every season no matter what it looks like. Know that he is working everything together for your good even if you don't understand it now. Trust him. He never stops breathing life into dry bones. He makes all things new!

Lord over all, you are always faithful. Thank you for never leaving me—not even for a moment. Fill me with your presence today and every day. You are the life in my soul: my joy, my hope, and the confidence of my heart. Walk with me as I journey on the path of your love.